WOMEN IN THE BIBLE:
A CONTEMPORARY PERSPECTIVE

Editor: Dr. Margie Lovett-Scott

with 17 Christian Contributing Authors

WGWPublishing.com

Copyright © Margie Lovett-Scott 2023

All Rights Reserved

ISBN: 979-8-9887355-3-3

All illustrations created by Bernard Lewis, Jr.

Final Edit: Wandah Gibbs, Ed. D.

Printed in the USA

WGW Publishing Inc.
621 Wellington Avenue,
Rochester NY 14619
(585) 245-0285

Dedication

This book is dedicated first and foremost to our Bible believing sisters who may not yet have had the opportunity to give voice to their stories as they journey through the Bible.

Also, to those who have yet to delve into the written word.

Finally, we encourage everyone, particularly women, to unapologetically share their stories with those in their networks as they diligently study God's word and spread the great news.

Acknowledgements

A special thank you to my son Mathew, for providing much needed support and encouragement in resolving some early, unexpected technical problems. Thanks also to Abena my accountant daughter, who really simplified the management of financial spreadsheets, so even I could understand them. Finally, kudos to Gloria Pipkins, a talented friend who worked her magic and resolved a major technical problem as I approached my final deadline.

Foreword

Women in the Bible: A Contemporary Perspective is another awesome rendition of what some may refer to as a: "Bible Study." However, Bible Study, is not necessarily the right term nor a completely comfortable fit for this work. As a seminary trained minister, it was a wonderful challenge for me to lay aside my tendency to do exegetical explorations and hermeneutical connections while reading about biblical personalities, their times and their situations. This contemporary perspective presents us with the challenge to simply flow with the stories as presented by each contributing author, keeping the woman whose story was shared in mind.

It is a refreshing departure to just read, reflect and meditate on the meaning of each story. As a woman, reading how God moved in the lives of biblical women and contemporary women alike is extremely uplifting. As I read and shared the stories, experienced the personal testimonies, and listened to and then answered the questions posed by each author, I became invigorated and even more motivated to continue along my Christian journey.

While not necessarily unique in its content, this work provides a significant opportunity for women to lift up their voices and speak their own truths. Though we live in the 21st century, women continue to struggle, not only to be heard, but heard in a way that is significant for the growth and development of the lives of all women.

Even though in the 21st century, our current society seems bent on pushing back the gains women have made in the last 100 years. This is particularly true for poor women, women of color (African, Latina, Asian/Pacific Islander descents, Indigenous Americans, Bi-Racial/Multi-Racial), and Seasoned (Senior) women. These contributing authors mapped out stories of biblical women in a way that doesn't just speak to the personal lives of women, it also depicts the foundation of the fundamental societal structures regarding gender. An issue which continues to challenge us even in contemporary times.

As a Christian Educator, Bible teacher, and minister, I offer *Women of the Bible: A Contemporary Perspective* to women and men alike who are determined to understand the challenges women face; not just as women, but as believers trying to live with Christian integrity.

Women of the Bible: A Contemporary Perspective, allows women to share their stories, bear each other's burdens and sorrows, share each other's joys and concerns, and encourage each other to become all that God in His infinite wisdom purposed for the lives of all women.

Rev. Dr. J. Esther Rowe, Rochester, New York

Table of Contents

Chapter	Page
Introduction	01
Abigail	05
Anna	11
Esther, Queen	17
Hagar	21
Hannah	29
Job's Wife	35
Jochebed	39
Judge Deborah	45
Lot's Wife	51
Lydia	57
Mary and Martha	63
Mary Magdalene	69
Mary Mother of Jesus	75
Noah's Wife	81
Priscilla	87
Queen of Sheba	93
Rahab	101

Rizpah	107
Ruth	115
Sarah	121
Tabitha (Dorcas)	127
The Servant Girls	135
The Woman at the Well	139
The Woman with the Issue of Blood	145
Vashti, Queen	151
Summary: A Final Look Back	157
References	161
Bibliography	167
Chapter Contributors	169
Scriptural References	175

Special Note to Our Readers

1. The chapters in this book are listed alphabetically.
2. All Biblical references in this book are from the King James Version of the Bible with exception of the following:

- ❖ Chapters 11, 16, and 18
- ❖ Chapter 11- Mary and Martha: New Revised Standard Bible (NRSV)
- ❖ Chapter 16 - Queen of Sheba: New International Version (NIV); New Revised Standard Bible (NRSV), and New Revised Study Bible (NRSB)
- ❖ Chapter 18 - Rizpah: New International Version (NIV)

3. Throughout this book, all direct references to God, or Jesus are capitalized pronouns such as He, Him, His...

4. The text in red, as in the Bible signifies Jesus' spoken words.

Deep River, my home is over Jordan:

I want to cross over into campground.

Deep River, my home is over Jordan:

Deep River, Lord, I want to cross over into campground.

O' don't you want to go to that Gospel feast,

That promised land where all is at peace?

O' Deep River, Lord, I want to cross over into campground.

Harry Thacker Burleigh, 1927

Chapter 1

Introduction

"Deep River Lord, I want to cross over into campground."
Harry Thacker Burleigh

The Bible represents the written word of God. However, most of us men and women, including Bible scholars, have but a cursory understanding of the women in the Bible. Rarely is there a brief mention of them included in a sermon, or in Bible study. Many Biblical women were silent, supporters of their husbands (warriors or rulers), others were servants, but most were outstanding.

The goal of this book is to encourage the reader to reflect on the written Biblical word and consider the era, environment, actual lived experiences, and circumstances of these women and think beyond the obvious Biblical word, to gain a broader perspective. In fact, some might liken many of the Biblical challenges to which we are most familiar as God's redemptive lessons, to prevent us from making the same or similar mistakes. The lesson, "if My people would just wake up, honor My word, do what is pleasing in My sight, and embrace this model daily, all will be well."

We all have audiences, not just among Christians but in the broader community; unsaved family, our workplaces, the store, the salon, the gym, and friends and neighbors to whom we should be witnessing about the goodness of God's word. No matter where we go, others are watching. Not always is spreading His word about what we say, but also about what we do. How we treat others matters most. Our behavior often speaks much louder than our words.

Most of the Biblical women discussed in this book are awesome demonstrations of devotion, loyalty, hard work, and determination who trusted in the Lord. An expectation of this book is to provide necessary insight resulting from challenges experienced by these women for application today. We encourage readers to reflect on their Christian journey as they strategize ways in which they might best maximize outcomes as they approach life's challenges and prepare their children to do the same.

Powerful, women in today's church, who are dedicated to serving God, and capable of furthering the mission of the church, are too often relegated to support roles. They lead the fundraising charge, the Mission, outreach programs, Sunday School, Vacation Bible School, tutoring programs, daycare, elder care, and special care of the Pastor and his Wife. It is fair to say the doors of the church would not remain open without the support of women. Yet, much like clergy who omit Biblical women from their sermons, and teachings, today's women are too often denied major church leadership roles. Women clergy have historically been banned from pulpits and devalued as equals. Why then, did God create woman in the first place? Was it not to provide a helpmate to the man? Why in some churches, are pastoring, and co-pastoring women, and pulpit associates, unwelcome?

This book addresses how some of the realities faced by women today parallel the trials and triumphs of the Biblical women discussed in this book. Many of us can find a reflection of ourselves experienced by the women depicted. It is hoped that the reader will apply some of the lessons learned from these Biblical women to their own lives and stay the course as they pave a life's journey that is truly pleasing in God's sight. For it is every Christian's dream of peace and hope on earth, to one day make it home to be with the Lord. The road will not be easy, as we all must go through some difficulties and conquer the deep waters of life before we make it to heaven, or campground, as so powerfully depicted by Burleigh.

Author: Margie Lovett-Scott

References

Burleigh, H.T. (1927). *Deep River.* New York: G. Ricordi and Co.

Abigail
- HOLDING THE
BREAD & FLOUR

Chapter 2

Abigail

"Beauty is nothing without brains and heart."
Karen Salmansohn

Abigail, an Israelite, was wise beyond her years. She was admired for being charming, loyal, beautiful, and smart. Her loyalty to God was paramount. Her strong historical Jewish knowledge, and love of God was commendable. Her husband, Nabal, was the opposite.

Despite being wealthy, Nabal was lauded as being foolish and evil (1 Samuel 25:3). His godless, angry, ruthless, and verbally abusive behavior probably accounted for him being widely disliked, even feared by others. Abigail appeared to silently, tolerate his foolishness, and drunkenness, and would likely today be described as a woman trapped in a tumultuous marriage without complaint.

David, a herdsman respected Saul the reigning king, despite his repeated attempts to kill him. However, when Saul and his men discovered David in a cave, the darkness of the cave gave David the advantage. He cut off a piece of Saul's robe but spared his life, as the Lord had placed Saul in the role of king (1 Samuel 24: 1-11).

David lived in the hills with about 600 followers, (1 Samuel 23:13) men who believed that David would one day be king. They generally assisted herdsmen in defending farm owners and townspeople's property from thieves and raiders. Their reward was customarily food and drink once the sheep were sheared.

Despite Nabal's knowledge of this practice, the 10 young men David sent to properly introduce themselves to Nabal, requesting food and drink on behalf of David, were turned away, and they returned empty handed (1 Samuel 25: 4-13).

David was angered at Nabal's refusal to help, despite the good he and his men had done in protecting his property and livestock. He told the men to bear arms and led about 400 of them to seek revenge. He intended to kill the unsuspecting, Nabal and his entire household, for refusing to provide supplies they had rightfully earned!

I believe it was divine intervention that one of the servants told Abigail all about what had happened, ensuring she knew it was only her husband at fault. The servant told her how David's men were always kind to them, even protected them day and night while they were in the fields. Immediately upon hearing the story, Abigail sprang into action. She quickly gathered "200 loaves, two bottles of wine, and five sheep ready dressed, five measures of parched *corn*, 100 clusters of raisins and 200 cakes of figs," which were securely packed onto donkeys without her husband's knowledge (1 Samuel 25: 14-19).

Abigail sent her servants ahead, following behind with all the food and drinks loaded onto the donkeys. She encountered David and his men enroute to her house. She immediately dismounted, fell at his feet signifying that he was her superior. She then apologized for her husband's behavior, begged for mercy, and asked that he accept her offerings and forgiveness.

Her quick thinking and actions avoided enormous bloodshed on both sides, which was certain to have occurred had she not acted so quickly. She also, witnessed to David that the Lord was well pleased with him, and because he had done no wrong throughout his life, God would always protect him even when others sought to kill him (1 Samuel 25:19-35). Can you imagine the outcome had David not listened to Abigail, or if he had missed her on the road? God had to be in the plans, or things would have turned out much differently.

Upon her return home, Abigail discovered that Nabal, unaware of the danger that had been averted, was hosting a huge party fit for a king. He was so drunk that it wasn't until the next morning that Abigail could tell him how she had averted a bloodbath. Upon hearing the story, he was stricken with a stone-like, heart ailment and 10 days later died, (1 Samuel 36-38). After Nabal's death Abigail married, David, the future King of Israel (1 Samuel 25:39-42).

Several lessons can be learned from Abigail's story. First, beauty is only skin deep, without soundness of mind it means nothing. Abigail had both beauty and brains. How about you, or those with whom you interact most closely?

Secondly, "Blessed are the peacemakers: for they shall be called the children of God." (Matthew 5: 9) Abigail was a peacemaker. What about you?

Thirdly, actions speak louder than words. Abigail wasted no time upon hearing about Nabal's actions. When your actions are backed with sound judgement as was the case for Abigail, you will usually win.

Finally, wealth is meaningless if you are unhappy, and don't know the Lord. Abigail appeared to be in an unfulfilling marriage. Although, her husband was wealthy, she hated his ungodly behavior, his evilness, and drunkenness. If this sounds familiar? Give it to God!

Author: Margie Lovett-Scott

References

King James Bible. (1990). Nashville: Thomas Nelson Publishers, Inc.

1 Samuel 23:13

Then David and his men, which were about six hundred, arose and departed out of Keilah, and went whithersoever they could go. And it was told Saul that David was escaped from Keilah; and he forbare to go forth.

Chapter 3

Anna the Widow and Prophet

"And there was one Anna, a prophetess...And she was a widow of about fourscore and four years,"
Luke 2:36a & 37a (KJV)

As we read the birth narratives of the Gospel of Luke, we come to a portion in chapter two that introduces Anna and describes her not only as a widow but also as a prophetess. Anna is said to be a descendent of Asher, one of Jacob called Israel's sons, through her father Phanuel's line. This would mean that Anna is from the Northern Kingdom or Northern Israel.

Anna married young and was married for seven years before becoming a widow. At the time we are introduced to Anna, she is said to be about 84 years old. Anna "departed not from the Temple but served God with fasting and prayers night and day" (Luke 2:37, NKJV). Anna spoke (prophesied) about Jesus when she encountered him with Mary and Joseph, "to all them that looked for redemption in Jerusalem" (Luke 2:38b, KJV).

Widows During Biblical Times

Generally, during biblical times, especially Old Testament times up through the coming of Jesus, the life and times of a widow were very hard. Widows very often suffered at the hands of the powerful. (Youngblood, p. 312). The best possible future for a widow lay in her remarrying, especially if she had no grown children or kin nearby. A widow might return to her father's house, or she might live with her mother-in-law (Tenny, p.928). There is a provision in the Mosaic Law called a "Levarite Marriage." Under certain circumstances, a brother or male next of kin should marry the widow (Deuteronomy 25:5-10). Similarly, Judah's preparation of his widowed daughter-in-law Tamar regarding the duty of the surviving brother (Genesis 38:11), (Tenny, p. 928). If a son was born from this marriage, he would be considered the deceased man's son.

A widow was made a special ward of the court based upon the theme that God Himself is the special protector of widows (Psalm 68:5), (Tenney, p. 928). Through Mosaic Law, God provided her with the opportunity to glean in the orchards and vineyards after the harvesters had taken most of the crop (Deuteronomy 24:19-22). The widow shared in the third-year tithe along with the Levites (Deut. 26:12), (Youngblood, p. 1312).

If a widow made a vow unto the Lord, the Mosaic Law considered the widow's vow binding. If she made the vow while married and her husband did not abolish it, it was considered binding. In this instance the widow was treated as a special legal person, equal to a man (Numbers 30), (Tenney, p. 928).

Reflections

Anna, who has a wonderful personality, is shared with us in the Gospel of Luke. She is unquestionably notable because of her steadfast devotion to God and her disciplined and consistent worship of Him. She is also notable because of her freedom of movement in the temple precincts and the fact that she is called a prophetess who undoubtedly also has the freedom to speak. Both these things were unusual for women during that era, especially, since she was not a priest nor a Levite. It is also important to note Anna's age, at 84, which means that she was full of years, experience, and wisdom.

Anna's importance in the Gospel of Luke is immeasurable. First, she is a woman in an extremely patriarchal and male dominated system of laws and government. Luke, however, is one gospel that deeply explores the relationship of women to the ministry of Jesus, and lifts women to a different perspective when speaking about ministry in its various forms. The fact that Anna is given the title of prophetess is significant because she carries on a long-standing tradition of women prophets in the Old Testament. In addition, Anna's role as prophet, particularly as she prophesies over Jesus, infers the leadership roles that women will assume in the early Church of Christ. It also implies that women as well as men will carry the message of Jesus the Christ.

It is no small thing that Anna committed herself to fasting and praying day and night. While we do not know the actual circumstances of her widowhood, it is evident that she has made a binding vow to the Lord and has remained committed to it during her life as a widow. We can assume that she did not remarry. If she had, unless she became widowed again, she would not be able to spend her time fasting and praying in the Temple. Her duties would be to her household and family.

Lessons Learned from Anna

- ❖ A widow can have a purpose and a goal beyond seeking remarriage.
- ❖ Seasoned (senior) women still have a role in the life of the community of believers. They never become obsolete.
- ❖ Women have significant roles to play in the ministry and mission of Jesus.
- ❖ Dedicated fasting and praying can lead to a life of spiritual power on behalf of the Lord.

Do you have, or have you had exposure to senior women in your community of believers? If so, in what way(s) do, or did they influence you or younger women and men in their presence?

Author: Rev. Dr. J. Esther Rowe

References

Liefeld, W.L. "Luke," In: Gaebelin, Frank E., Gen. Ed. The Expositer's Bible Commentary. Volume 8. Grand Rapids, MI: Zondervan, 1984, pp 818-1059.

King James Bible. (1986). Nashville: Thomas Nelson Publishers

Schaberg, J. "Luke," In: Newsom, Carol A and Sharon H Ringe, Eds. The Women's Bible Commentary. Louisville: Westminster/John Knox Press, 1992, pp 275-292.

Tenney, M.C., Gen. Ed. The Zondervan Pictorial Encyclopedia of the Bible. Volume 5 Q-Z. Grand Rapids: Zondervan, 1975, 1976.

Youngblood, RF., Gen. Ed. Nelson's New Illustrated Bible Dictionary. Completely Revised and Updated Edition. Nashville: Thomas Nelson Publishers, 1995, 1986.

ESTHER, QUEEN

Chapter 4

Esther

"It is my commandment, That ye love one another, as I have loved you. Greater love hath no man than this, that a man lay down his life for his friends."
John 15:12-13

Esther was courageous during a time of national crisis, but not before she fasted and prayed to God for His guidance. There is a popular saying, that beauty is only skin deep. In Esther's case, her cousin Mordecai, who raised her as his own daughter after she became orphaned (Esther 2:7), made certain that Esther's beauty was not the focus of her life. However, neither of them could have known how radically their lives would change. After all, they were captives in the land of the Medes and the Persians. Mordecai, of the tribe of Benjamin (v. 5) was a devout and committed follower of God and he privately and publicly lived accordingly.

While King Ahasuerus' (Xerxes I 485-464 B.C.) kingdom was more compassionate than most captors in the fourth century, the Jewish people had no rights. Although, they were not free to do as they pleased, they were allowed to worship their God in this foreign land.

Esther was an obedient "daughter" for Mordecai and trusted his judgment as they both served in this pagan kingdom. Hearing the news that the king was searching for a new queen; she didn't run to Mordecai and say, "I want to compete because I'm pretty enough (v.7); we can have a better life if I win and become queen." Isn't that what 21st century society advertises to beautiful young girls, looking only at outward appearances, the glamour enticements and prizes? We can only presume that she didn't think that way because through the centuries, Jewish parents, children, and strangers with them, were admonished to hear and learn and to "fear the LORD your God and observe to do all the words of this law" (Deuteronomy 31:12).

While, becoming queen was not Esther's desire, Mordecai recognized that God might be up to something. GOD is not mentioned in the Book of Esther, but we can see His divine providence as the events unfold. Mordecai instructed Esther to show up with the other maidens to be considered but not to reveal her heritage (brought up Hadassah...the daughter of Abihail), not yet (Esther 2:7,15). Esther was then chosen queen of Persia. Everything is based on God's timing, not ours.

Now there was an enemy among them, Haman, the Agagite, who had a plan of his own. Have you noticed that sometimes things seem too good to be true? It's not unusual for people native to a land to resent strangers in their community who they believe are living off them and gaining more recognition than them. Haman let his hatred for Mordecai blind him, causing him and his sons to lose their lives. Is hate worth losing your life for? "What shall a man profit if he gains the whole world and loses his soul?"

After learning about the plot that Haman had devised to annihilate her people, Esther vows: "and If I perish, I perish" (Esther 4:16), but I'm going to see the king." The matter was bigger than just her family. As God delivered Gideon, "Oh my Lord, wherewith shall I save Israel?" (Judges 6:15), He shows up for Esther too and all the Jewish people in the 127 provinces of Persia and the palace of Shushan are saved. Obedience brought victory to all, reminding us that, God uses ordinary people to do extraordinary things. Be obedient to God and leave the consequences to Him.

Author: Cheryl A. Pough

References

King James Bible. (1994). Nashville: Thomas Nelson Publishers

Hagar –
Battered & Pregnant

Chapter 5

Hagar

"Never trust your fears, they don't know your strength."
Athena Singh

A Mother's Dusty Road

The Book Genesis is filled with divine history. It is the key to opening our understanding and relationship with God. Woman, made during the six days of creation to be a helpmate, became much more. We know Abram and Sarai spent time in Egypt and were headed to Canaan. Little is known about the giver or why, but Hagar, the Egyptian slave maiden was gifted to them, and became Sarai's maid.

Before Abram even left Egypt, he believed in the Lord. His faith was unquenchable, but two things caused him trouble; he was very wealthy, and he took Hagar, the Egyptian maid (McGee, 1981). God had promised a child to Abram and Sarai. Because the pregnancy took much longer than Sarai desired, she executed her plan to give Hagar to Abram, which he did not reject.

A closer look at Hagar and women of the Bible reveals that although men outnumber women in terms of Biblical stories, it does not negate the importance of women particularly, in stories regarding Jesus.

Jewish and Christian traditions solidified the treatment of women during these times (Packer and Tenny, 1980). Past chaos between culture and religion is reflected today by major bickering over the role of women in a man's world, and the stereotyping of appropriate versus inappropriate behavior. This is particularly, true of how Black woman are often wrongfully viewed by other cultures as, angry, aggressive, domestic, uneducated, and promiscuous baby makers. Although not widely publicized, it remains a stereotypical viewpoint of far too many. A major aspect of politics in America today seeks to control a woman's reproductive rights.

During Biblical times, not only were women treated unfairly, but they were also more likely to be poor, oppressed foreigners forced to submit to powerful nations. Akin, to the treatment of women in the Ukraine and Iran; raped, killed and discarded under the guise of war. Nothing changed in man's behavior for generations, attested to by such notable women as Harriet Tubman and Sojourner Truth as they sought to do God's will. Also evidenced by the relationship between Sally Hemings and Thomas Jefferson whose daughter punished Hemings by forcing her to nurse her children.

Hagar's plight as a victim of circumstances, abuse, and sexual submission, a foreigner, aimlessly, traveling that dusty road to wherever it took her was similar. She had no rights and had to submit not only to her mistress' demands but also, the husband's. The culture and society of that time treated women like Hagar as second-class citizens at best. The spiritual truth was that Hagar was just as holy and important in the eyes of God (Trigilio and Brighenti, 2005). Hagar had great wisdom and exercised good judgement especially when she listened to the voice of God.

As the story goes, Sarai now well beyond childbearing age wanted to quickly produce a son and fulfill the promise of God. She did not cherish God's promise. She gives her most valuable possession to her husband so she can produce a child (Genesis 16:1-3). This was not an action of bad faith on Sarai's behalf. Rather, it was a sacrifice of husband and love for a nation. In fact, in Ur, their original hometown, there were many concubines utilized for childbearing. God did not approve of this practice, nor did He approve of Hagar being given to Abram. It was Sarai's idea, but Abram complied, an action perhaps fueled by his previous lie that Sarai was his sister (Genesis, 20:1-11).

Hagar's Boastfulness

Hagar becomes pregnant with Abram's seed. She boasts, "I've mothered a child that Abram and Sarai could not" (McGee, 1981), and she looks down on Sarai. This young woman had been taken from her native land, abused by her guardian, then submitted to a man for the sole purpose of bearing his child. Why wouldn't she laud that over her mistress as it obviously got her points with the husband who now had an heir. People tend to boast about their gifts despite how they got them.

Women of color have traveled similar dusty roads, boasting in search of solace. It doesn't pay! In these United States, women of lighter complexion once boasted over darker complexioned women who had to work out in the hot sun or under horrible conditions. Black women today have grown to understand that we are as one in the sight of God no matter how dark or light our skin is, or how nappy our hair. Sarai sees that she has done wrong by not trusting God to fulfill His promise in providing an heir. Her actions, though wrong, were common practice in those days. But it was their unbelief that was especially displeasing in God's sight. It was sinful.

Hagar Flees Down the Path Least Taken

No longer able to take the abuse from Sarai, Hagar, though pregnant in a foreign land, sets off towards unknown territory. Death for her and her unborn child was imminent had it not been for divine intervention of a God sent angel. Perhaps this was the incarnate Christ, always looking out for the lost. Hagar heeds the advice and wisdom of the angel and returns to her mistress to protect her unborn child. The angel shares a promise, which Hagar stores in her heart, indicating that her seed would be multiplied. She would become the matriarch of a nation through the birth of her son, Ishmael (Galatians 4:22-31).

Paul later uses this as an allegory (McGee, 1981). He speaks of Hagar and her child as being Mount Sinai where Mosaic Law was given, which speaks of the legality and bondage of that law. It later proves to be a great sorrow for Abram. Hagar returns and gives birth to Ishmael, "because the Lord hath heard thy affliction." The angel had also shared with Hagar that her son would be a wild man, (Genesis 16:11-12), as if preparing her to witness her son in battle. Look at the Middle East today, in constant battle, numerous accounts of widespread suffering, women being publicly raped, murdered, and oppressed.

After the birth of Sarai's son Isaac, friction escalated in the household between Sarai and Hagar's sons. At Sarai's demand, Abram gives Hagar minimal rations and sends them away. Hagar again, finds herself on a dusty road, now with a small child. Meager rations all but gone, and realizing there is no one to save her, she places him under a shrub and wanders away. The child starts crying and the voice of God is there to save the lost, once more (Genesis 21:12-20).

Envy and jealousy are difficult to forgive when you are constantly being abused and mistreated. However, God who sees all, was with her, a source of assurance. A mother's love for her child will always trump oppression and maltreatment when you hearken to the voice of God. Hagar was a strong black woman who survived a foreign land, hatred, degradation, exploitation, and hardships just as many of our ancestors did, and are still doing. Hagar is not a victim, but a survivor (Spangler and Syswerda, 2007).

Author: Easter G. Tucker

References

McGee, V. J. (1981). Thru the Bible, Vol. I, Nashville: Thomas Nelson Publishers,

Packer, J.I., and Tenny, M.C. eds. (1980) Illustrated Manners and Customs of the Bible. Nashville, TN: Thomas Nelson Publishers.

Roe vs. Wade, 410 U.S. 113, United States Supreme Court. January 22, 1973.

Spangler, A. and Syswerda, J.E. (2007). Women of the Bible. Grand Rapids: Zondervan.

Trigilio, J. and Brighenti, K. (2005). Women in the Bible for Dummies. Hoboken: Wiley Publishing, Inc.

HANNAH
– LOOKING UP
PRAYING

Chapter 6

Hannah

"When the heart is right, the mind and body will follow."
Coretta Scott King

Hannah, the first of Elkanah's two wives encouraged him to take a second wife because she was barren. He did so as this was common practice during Biblical times and is still practiced in some cultures today.

As I think about Hannah, three things come to mind, the problem, the promise, and God's response to a prophetic prayer.

The Problem

Hannah like many women during Biblical times was a woman who found herself in a desperate situation. She could not bear children as she was infertile. Although her husband showed her the greatest amount of love, the humiliation she felt for being unable to have a child caused her much pain and agony for years. The very thought of being childless absolutely caused the greatest sorrow for Hannah.

Imagine a woman whose womb appeared to be closed, who desperately yearned to have a child and everyday endured great agony and severe ridicule from others. As a woman of God (Genesis 1:28), "Be fruitful and multiply," perhaps brought even greater agony for Hannah.

The Vow/the Prophetic words

In life, many situations bring mockery from others. In this case, Peninnah ridicules Hannah whose husband is perplexed by her agony. In fact, Elkanah's love for Hannah far surpasses his love for Peninnah. However, unaware of the mockery, he is unable to understand what Hannah is going through. Despite Hannah's bitterness, pain, and barrenness, she pushes herself forward and makes a vow, (1 Samuel 1:10-11). Hannah asks God for a son and vows that if her gift is granted, she'll give him back to God. This situation required a true heart transformation and an internal face toward God. Hannah's desire was that God would not only hear, but also understand the cry of her heart.

My personal story is I too, was barren for several years and like Hannah endured countless individuals asking me, "what are you waiting for to have a child?" I prayed to God, and with my unwavering faith and sincere belief that I would receive a child, God delivered. Today, my first born, a daughter, is 27 years of age and like Hannah, I gave her back to God the minute she was born. Again, like Hannah, two years later He blessed me abundantly, by giving me a son, who I also gave back to Him.

The Promise

Often, we waste precious time and energy searching far and wide for help from others; a friend, relative, co-worker, or church member, before finally coming to the realization that we only need the one person who truly understands what we're going through. Who better to turn to than God?

Hannah needed to find inner peace and someone who could truly understand her pain. Eli the priest, in (1 Samuel 1:17), tells Hannah to, "go in peace: and the God of Israel grant *thee* thy petition that thou hast asked of Him."

Hannah's story ends with the promise of God fulfilled because He heard her cry just as He hears our cries and gives us the desires of our heart. I am a living witness and can truly understand Hannah's position, her pain, her sorrow, her vow, and God's promises.

Have you ever relinquished all your doubts and truly waited on the Lord? Hannah did! Though frustrated, discouraged, ridiculed, perhaps even bullied by others? No matter what we go through in life, like Hannah, pray about it, put all your faith in God, and wait on a miraculous solution.

Lessons learned from Hannah:

Seek God first. Hannah did and He blessed her. *Thank him for the blessing received*, as she did. *Be true to your word,* demonstrated by giving her son back to God. She took him to Shiloh for religious training and study. Because Hannah kept her word she was blessed abundantly, beyond anything imaginable. She eventually had five children: three sons, and two daughters (1 Samuel 2:21). Although not much is known about Samuel's other siblings, Samuel became one of the most prominent, anointed, spiritual leaders in Israel, later anointing the first two kings of Israel: Saul, and David.

    Can you imagine what may have happened had Hannah not kept her promise to God after receiving her first blessing? Can you recall a time when you kept a promise and were rewarded, or broke a promise and experienced serious turmoil? What might you do differently, based on this story?

Author: Joanne Mitchell-McLaren

References

King James Bible. YouVersionBibleApp (2016). Edmond: Life.Church. Downloaded. November 2017.

I Samuel 2:21

And the Lord visited Hannah, so that she conceived, and bare three sons and two daughters. And the child Samuel grew before the Lord.

Job's Wife
- Frustrated
- Sickness

Chapter 7

Job's Wife

"It's pretty hard for the Lord to guide you if you haven't made up your mind which way to go."
Madam C.J. Walker

Job's wife, alleged to be named Dinah, reminds me of the old gospel hymn, "...Great is thy Faithfulness. Morning by morning new mercies I see. All I have needed thy hand hath provided..." (Chisholm, 1923). Dinah witnessed her husband's demise, and both their lives falling apart. They experienced failing health and were pushed to the depths of despair. She then lost her children, their wealth, and property. Then to top it off, she witnessed her previously strong, courageous, husband's frailty. His nearly destroyed mental health, had a major effect on her and her children, not to mention her lifestyle.

Life as she knew it was over. Seeing him like that devastated her. At their lowest point she challenges Job to curse God and die. She was undoubtedly overwhelmed and upset that God would turn his back on his most righteous, faithful and devoted servant. Much like Lot's wife, she was touted as being very unsupportive. I would propose she was most likely so devastated that she had a momentary lapse of her senses.

Job, one of God's most faithful servants, despite being tested to the limit by the devil, trusted God so much that he refused to give up on Him. He remained convinced that if he held on for just a little while longer God would show up. I can only imagine God's voice as He repeatedly spoke to Job throughout this nightmare of a life, reassuring him every step of the way, to not give up, nor become discouraged. I imagine Job pleading with his wife to try and understand.

Both their lives had been turned upside down. All their possessions were gone; the enemy had all but consumed them both. Now, his wife, also ill, was an emotional wreck. She cried and pleaded all day with him to stop the pain and suffering and give up. No doubt she could no longer bear to see him suffering so, and perhaps to her, death appeared imminent as well. Finally, she was undoubtedly feeling desperate and deserted, thinking God had abandoned the one person in the world who had unrelenting faith in Him. It devastated her to see her loved one suffering so she dismissed all reasoning and challenged her husband to curse God and die. Can you relate to a situation or circumstance of any kind that could plunge a person so deeply into despair that they stop believing, and simply give up wishing the nightmare to be over? I believe that's the situation from which Job's wife was operating.

The lesson Job demonstrated throughout this ordeal, is that no matter how bleak things appear, how low you've sunk, or how hopeless the situation seems, do not give up. He reminds us that just as you approach your darkest hour, and feel like you're losing your grip on life, God will show up. I imagine, Job was hanging by a thread of life, when he heard the voice of God saying, "... I will never leave thee, nor forsake thee" (Hebrews 13:5). Trust in me I will show up, and I have great plans for you. Please don't give up. Hold on Job, for just a little while longer.

Continue to pray without ceasing. Keep calling out the name of the Lord and persist in rebuking the devil. For, if you are truly one of God's faithful servants, and have been true to His word and kept His commandments; just when you think life is over, the Lord miraculously steps in and presto, the devil flees. The predator who was trying to rip out your heart has fled, and just like that you are restored. Reflect on Job's story but remember his wife! Think about this story when you are faced with your next life-changing battle, especially if you have not yet, made up your mind to follow the path that leads to Christ.

Author: Margie Lovett-Scott

References

Chisholm, T. (1923). Great is Thy Faithfulness, Song. Hope Publishing (Based on Lamentations 3:23)

King James Bible. (1990). Nashville: Thomas Nelson Publishers

Jochebed

Chapter 8

Jochebed

"They are new every morning: great is thy faithfulness."
Lamentations 3:23

Jochebed, was a Hebrew woman of great courage and faith, and an early believer in, "it takes a village to raise a child." Though pregnant with baby Moses, she positioned herself for the unknown.

Destined by Pharaoh's decree that all male babies born to Hebrew women were to be thrown into the Nile to drown, meant she had to act quickly. Helpless and defenseless, other women might've simply given up. Not Jochebed however because she trusted God implicitly.

Jochebed's story speaks to all women, mothers, grandmothers, sisters, aunties, and sister girls. When you really think about it, we're all women of the Bible, a written living legacy of history and purpose, passed on to each of us at the beginning of creation.

The Bible tells us: "And the rib, which the LORD God had taken from the man, made he a woman, and brought her unto the man. And Adam said, 'This *is* now bone of my bones, and flesh of my flesh: she shall be called Woman,' ..." (Genesis 2: 22-23). God created woman to nurture and be a vessel of wisdom. She was intended to be a leader in her family and in her community, and to have a passionate relationship with Him.

Are Women Special to God?

Contrary to popular opinion, God constantly lets us know how He feels about Woman, His creation. He chose women to bring life into this world. He chose and trusted a woman to birth His only son, and care for Him. Women demonstrate over and over that they are equipped to carry the heavy load of life's emotional and physical stress. Hello Sojourner Truth, hello Harriet Tubman, and **hello Jochebed!**

When we lean on and trust in God, we can raise children, work a full-time job, take care of a husband, work in our community, and be a caregiver. Women are awesome! How do we do it? We do it by reflecting on one day at a time. Like Jochebed, we understand there's a force greater than us, and He works on our behalf. When we do our part, the Lord will certainly do His. He even tells us, "Take therefore no thought for the morrow: for the morrow shall take thought for the things of itself..." (Matthew 6:34). "O taste and see that the LORD *is* good: ..." (Psalm 34:8). What can we learn from Jochebed?

Jochebed: A daughter of Levi, the wife of Amram, the mother of Moses, Miriam, and Aaron. She was no different than the rest of us. Jochebed had storms, struggles and obstacles in her life, including the oppression of slavery and by being a woman. You know what I'm talking about, we've all been there before. When situations seem hopeless and there appears to be no answer or no end in sight, where do we turn? Remember Jochebed was enslaved and had no rights, no power and no authority. Does that sound familiar?

Jochebed's Trust, Faith and Relationship with God

Pharaoh put forth a decree that all Hebrew males were to be killed at birth. But, Jochebed had no fear. She knew there had to be a solution. There's a song that says, "I found the answer, I learned to pray with Faith to guide me I found the way." Jochebed was a strong woman, already anchored in the Solid Rock which was God! She was prayed UP!

"By faith Moses, when he was born, was hid three months by his parents, because they saw *he was* a proper child; and they were not afraid of the kings' commandment." (Hebrews 11:23) Meaning, Moses was born different from the other children. He was born anointed with special qualities. You see, God has a purpose for our lives before we're even born. Pharaoh's daughter found Moses floating in the Nile. Although he was provided safe refuge during his childhood, "By faith Moses, when he was come to years, refused to be called the son of Pharaoh's daughter" (Hebrews 11:24). I believe God was already working out Jochebed's problem while Moses was still in the womb.

A friend who is a woman of great faith, described it this way; "Faith in God is the only WAY, it's that small, still Voice that speaks to you when you really need it" (Latimer-Hunt). Finally, the Bible says, "Now faith is the substance of things hoped for, the evidence of things not seen" (Hebrews 11:1). Faith is golden, sometimes we simply need to wait on God for direction.

I leave with you this question. Where are you in your Faith? Are you a Jochebed?

Author: Martha Hope

References

King James Bible. (1990). Nashville: Thomas Nelson Publishers, Inc.

Latimer-Hunt, A. (n.d.) Memorial AME Zion Church. Prior First Lady's sacred message of encouragement.

Psalm 34: 8

O taste and see that the Lord is good: blessed *is* the man *that* fear him.

Deborah

- Judge & Prophetess
- Warrior who went to battle

Chapter 9

Judge Deborah

*"I can do all things through Christ
which strengtheneth me."*
Philippians 4:13 (KJV)

Deborah, known for her strong faith, was a notable judge, prophetess, courageous leader, wife, and ruler. She was highly respected and well sought out during times of trouble, and she was the brains behind numerous victories. Deborah, a military leader, could have led Israel to victory over the Canaanites. Instead, honoring God's request she successfully, assisted the hesitant and weaker General Barak.

Deborah also known as (Devorah or D'vorah) Hebrew meaning "bee" (Ryan, 2021; McClain-Walters, 2015). Her leadership, wisdom and courage have contributed to many devotionals, seminars, and sermons. She was the only female judge to lead God's chosen people, the Israelites, successfully into battle. She was also, a poet and gifted sharer of God's word. I'm not sure many are aware of her incredible singing and songwriter talents.

God Challenges Us

As judge, she was responsible for judging the Israelites. After blatant wrongdoing and repeatedly asking God for forgiveness, they fell back into evilness, idolatry and disobedience.

Deborah summoned Barak, from Kedesh-Naphtali, and questioned his ignoring of God's command to take 10,000 men into battle against King Jabin's army at Mount Tabor. Though God promised him he'd be victorious, Barak fearing failure against the fearless captain Sisera, would only go if Deborah went with him. She agreed, but not before warning him that he would not be honored for the victory because of his weak faith. Instead, victory would be at the hands of a woman (Judges 4: 4-9).

With numerous challenges and unrest in the world today, it's easy to empathize with Deborah who also lived through challenging times. Deborah encouraged others to stand up and fight. When leaders lead, others will follow. Could today be the day that God calls you to do more than you ever imagined for His Kingdom? Don't think God will not use YOU. Be inspired that He uses ordinary people to accomplish extraordinary things. He wants you to realize all that He has planned for you.

Following God's Call

On an ordinary day 33 years ago, God called me to work at an acute care hospital. This call came after comfortably working and doing well for years in long-term care. The thought of moving to an unfamiliar acute care position was not even on my radar until God began tugging at me to take the position. Being a single parent, my hesitancy was compounded by the fact that I was raising my daughter with the support of my family and her father's parents. However, I didn't want to be a problem or take advantage of their kindness.

Despite my uneasiness, and after praying and seeking God's guidance, I realized that if it was meant to be then everything would work out just fine. God gave me the courage to accept the night shift position in question.

He later provided a path for numerous educational opportunities, allowing me to earn advanced degrees and credentials. I began working in roles I had only dreamed about. Now, authoring peer-reviewed articles, speaking internationally, impacting patient care, nursing education, community health and wellness is routine for me.

I've advanced from LPN to RN and earned two master's degrees and a Doctorate. I get chills when I recall how God guided me every step of the way through many leadership journeys. He encouraged me with His word, strengthened me, and moved me to where He needed me to be. God had a plan and equipped me with soldiers to achieve outcomes that matter.

Recently, He did it again. I left my employment after 33 years of service. My journey was not straight nor obstacle free. When your foundation is built on integrity, unwavering faith in God, honesty, courage, and on doing what is best for the greater good, you cannot allow obstacles to hinder you. Not jealousy, envy, racism, genderism, nothing will prevent you from doing what you know is right. I'm blessed to have an amazingly, supportive husband of over 20 years, great parents, a brother, a daughter, a granddaughter, wonderful in-laws, friends, and colleagues. Also, whenever doubt surfaced, a Bible verse would interrupt my thoughts and give me strength and courage: "Fear thou not; for I *am* with thee: be not dismayed; for I *am* thy God: I will strengthen thee; yea, I will help thee; yea, I will uphold thee with the right hand of my righteousness" (Isaiah 41:10).

Stepping out on faith isn't always easy. When God gives us the strength to lead, He promises to be with us and do through us more than we can imagine for His Kingdom and His glory. Have you ever considered how God may be calling you to take on a leadership role? The same way, God used Deborah, He is calling you to courageously lead others to fight in His army.

Deborah's final legacy reads, "And the land had rest forty years," (Judges 5:31). Her faith-filled, courageous life brought peace to her people. Today, the way to peace is found in fulfilling God's plan for us. Let this be your legacy. The battle belongs to the Lord.

What lessons can we learn from Deborah, this amazing woman of the Bible? Her faith, courage, and leadership were catalysts for profound change and opportunity.

Author: Deborah Stamps

References

King James Bible. (1971). Nashville: Thomas Nelson Publishers, Inc.

McClain-Walters, M. (2015). The Deborah anointing: Embracing the call to be a woman of wisdom and discernment. Lake Mary: Charisma House Book Group

Ryan, J. (2021, June 16). 7 Lessons we can learn from Deborah in the Bible. Retrieved September 10, 2022, from https://www.crosswalk.com/faith/bible-study/lessons-we-can-learn-from-deborah-in-the-bible.html

LOT'S WIFE
- A pillar of salt is all left behind
- Where's my wife?

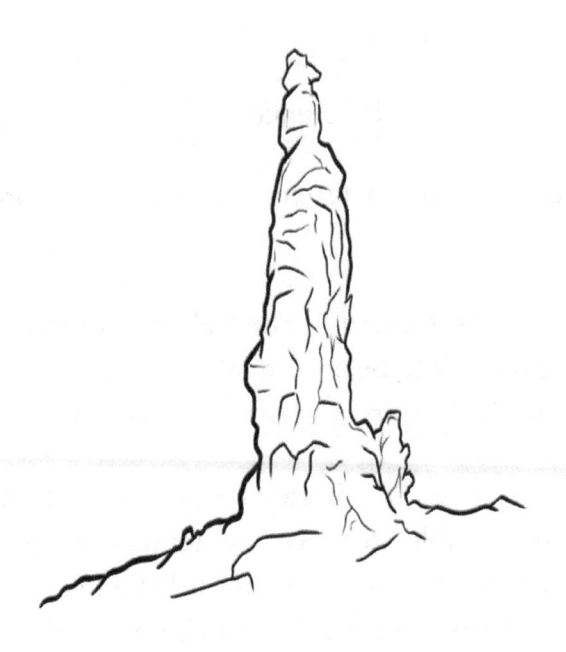

Chapter 10

Lot's Wife

"Never look back darling, it distracts from the now."
Edna Mode

Most know the Genesis 19, story of Sodom and Gomorrah, which I call the "Twin Sin Cities." There, people faced corruption of all sorts and on every level and risked being consumed by every imaginable sin. Abraham, commissioned by the Lord to find 50 righteous men in Sodom, in order to save the city from God's wrath, had failed his mission. After repeatedly, but unsuccessfully renegotiating with God to find a lowly 10 righteous men to save Sodom, he failed yet again. Finally, the Lord sent two angels to examine the situation.

Lot, knowing how corrupt and unsafe the city was, insisted on sheltering the angels in his own home, believing it to be the only safe haven in town. However, before retiring for the night, Lot found his home surrounded by evil men of Sodom. They had the dirtiest intentions imaginable (to rape and sodomize the angels). Lot went outside to reason with them but couldn't keep the mob at bay. Acknowledging the danger, the angels pulled Lot into the house, and caused blindness to overcome the mob. This allowed Lot, his wife and their daughters to escape before the Lord destroyed both cities.

They were given strict instructions to move quickly to the safety of the distant village and warned never to look back. Ironically, the men to which Lot's virgin daughters were betrothed refused to leave and were destroyed as the cities were burned to the ground, perhaps explaining their later evil actions toward their father (Genesis 19:30-36).

As Lot and his family approached the small village, that was to be their refuge, his wife glanced back towards Sodom. She was married to a powerful, influential and highly respected man. Perhaps in a flash of reluctancy to have relinquished her comfortable lifestyle and status, or maybe in hopes of simply getting a glimpse of family members she hoped were following behind, she looked back. In a split second she was turned into a pillar of salt. Therein ends her story.

Condemned for disobedience for just one glance! Many criticized her for disobeying God as instructed by the angels, others contend that because she was refusing to follow her husband, she was an unbeliever. Some say she may even have been desirous of adopting the lifestyle of wickedness they'd left behind. If so, this begs the question; can a devoted Christian live among that level of corruption? Can they mix daily with ungodly people without succumbing to the lifestyle they were trying to avoid?

I contend that she willingly left Sodom with her husband and two daughters, with no desire to return. She was not pulling away, nor walking or running in the opposite direction. Rather, she and her family were already approaching the distant village to which they were instructed to flee. Perhaps she hoped to get a glimpse of family following closely behind. Maybe she wanted one more look at the life she had willingly left behind, before beginning her new life in this distant village. No question, God knows our heart, and knows what we're thinking before we act. So, He also, knew her heart.

A closer look might cause one to question, whether God was indeed condemning her for being disobedient as many Bible scholars claim. Or was she perhaps being memorialized? If so, for what reason(s)?

Salt as depicted in the Bible is a good thing. The Bible tells us that salt sends a message of purification, value, and permanence. It is written in the Word, "Ye are the salt of the earth: ..." (Matthew 5:13). Today, we are saved by Grace and when we sin, we need do nothing more than confess (1 John 1:9). Once forgiven, we should put forth our best effort and try harder to give God our best.

Consider the women in your life who you believe are devout Christians, living unblemished lives. How many of these women do you believe have ever thought about doing, or did something they knew was wrong? Do you think they should be condemned or criticized for it? Do you believe that Christians who strive daily to walk the walk, and talk the talk, but periodically fall short should be criticized, or ostracized for their missteps? How about when you fall short? Have you been criticized, seen social media posts about you, leaving you embarrassed, outraged, or devastated? Maybe you left a situation you looked back at, or even went back to, though you repeatedly vowed you'd never do so again. Were you criticized by family or friends? It is impossible for anyone to really understand the reasons why people behave as they do, unless of course, they have walked a mile in that person's shoes.

Author: Margie Lovett-Scott

References

King James Bible. (1990). Nashville: Thomas Nelson Publishers, Inc.

Genesis 19: 31-32

And the firstborn said unto the younger, Our father is old and there is not a man in the earth to come in unto us after the manner of all the earth. Come, let us make our father drink wine, and we will lie with him, that we may preserve seed of our father.

Lydia
- Wealthy Business Women, sold purple cloth.

Chapter 11

Lydia of Thyatira: A Woman of Vision

"For where your treasure is, there will your heart be also."
Matthew 6:21, (KJV)

Most Bible readers are familiar with the basic facts about Lydia who is introduced to us in Acts Chapter 16. Lydia, a Gentile citizen of Thyatira, was living in Philippi when she first encountered the apostles Paul and Silas and their missionary team. We are further able to determine, from the brief Biblical narrative, that she was a wealthy and generous homeowner. She was head of household who had servants, possibly a widow, a successful businesswoman, and a dealer of Tyrian purple garments. However, much like us, there is more to Lydia's story than meets the eye. We certainly are more than our name, more than a title, where we're from, and more than the nature or circumstances of our birth.

Lydia had a clear vision which was written on her heart, and she found a way to appropriately act on it. Today, we often allow distractions to inhibit us from moving beyond our visions. A lesson from my mother reminds me of Lydia the visionary. When my siblings and I were kids, we loved to watch the *I Love Lucy Show* or *Shirley Temple* specials. We would sit for hours, thoroughly riveted to the black and white screen. If we dared to protest when Mom called us to dinner or to complete a particular chore, she would remind us that "Lucy's doing what Lucy's got to do." In other words, we needed to be about the business at hand, and carry out our assigned task, or mission. Even today, when I'm procrastinating or mindlessly engrossed, or become sidetracked, I am reminded of my mother's wise mantra.

Today, we're better positioned to identify our visions, and more clearly act on them. Using various self-reflection techniques and life application visuals we can bring our vision to life. These include utilizing faith-based vision boards. Creating such boards, as tangible expressions of prayer, reflecting our God-given promises, hopes, and dreams (Fort, 2011; Green Brown, 2016). Faith-based records of our vision can help center our focus and more fully utilize our abilities, senses, and gifts (Isaak, 2020). The Bible encourages us to write the vision and make it plain, "And the Lord answered me and said, Write the vision, and make *it* plain upon tables, that he may run that readeth it" (Habakkuk 2:2, KJV). In other words, if the recordings are clear, it enables the reader to act.

Lydia knew her mission, her task and she was committed to its fulfillment. She had hopes and dreams which included a vision of being included in Kingdom plans and purposes that were written in her heart by God and actualized by the works of her hands.

"And a certain woman named Lydia, a seller of purple, of the city of Thyatira which worshipped God, heard *us:* whose heart the Lord opened, that she attended unto the things which were spoken of Paul" (Acts 16:14). This scripture demonstrates that the Lord had opened Lydia's heart to listen to what Paul was telling her.

The work of Lydia's hands as a dealer of purple as well as through her acts of benevolent hospitality was favorably blessed and multiplied back to her. Have you ever asked God to favor you and bless the work of your hands? Lydia clearly did.

Consider that the production of purple dye was a smelly and labor-intensive business. Yet, Lydia was able to make that trade work for her. Out of the murex shellfish's excrement (Bond, 2017) purple dye was produced which was literally worth its weight in gold (Olesen, 2013; Cartwright, 2016).

Like Lydia, we may have been handed the muck of life, but we hold on to our God-given vision. We believe and receive the word of the Lord found in Romans 8:28, "And we know that all things work together for good to them that love God, to them who are the called according to His purpose." We've been blessed today to not only write, but also artistically create and record the visions we're determined to hear, receive, and act upon.

Lydia never lost sight of her vision and positioned herself to hear the good news of the gospel. She received and treasured it in her heart and then acted upon it. Heartfelt desires planted by God enabled Lydia to create a visionary model for Christian hospitality and the beginning of evangelistic house churches. In other words, Lydia took what she had and placed it in the Master's hands, then actualized the treasures of her heart.

Author: Dr. Corrine Houser

References

Bond, SE. (2017, Oct. 24). The hidden labor behind the luxurious colors of purple and indigo. Retrieved November 26, 2022, from hyperallergic.com: https://hyperallergic.com

Cartwright, M. (2016, July 21). Tyrian purple. Retrieved November 4, 2022, from World History Encyclopedia: https://www.worldhistory.org

Fort, C. (2011). What the Bible says about creating Vision Boards + An expressive therapeutic art prompt. Retrieved November 14, 2022, from https://12tribesministries.com

Green Brown, C. (2016, January 12). Visual prayer: How to create a spiritual Vision Board. San Diego: Dream Life Foundation

King James Bible Online. (1987). Retrieved November 29, 2022, from https://www.biblegateway.com

Isaak, K. (2020, January 20). Should Christians make Vision Boards and set goals? Retrieved November 4, 2022, from https://love motherblog.com/podcastepisode20/

Olesen, J. (2013). Color meanings – The power and symbolism of colors Retrieved November 2, 2022 from https://color-meanings.com

Mary, Where is Martha?

Chapter 12

Martha and Mary

"African American Females & the Imago Dei: Reclaiming God's Vision of Wholeness"
Jill F. Bradway

Sister, I thought you had my back?!!
Luke 10:38-422 (NRSV)

The relationship between sisters is special. A sister can be biological or borne out of adversity or adventure. The bond between sisters can be strong and positive or weakened by complicated interactions.

Martha was a woman on a mission. She was preparing for her most important guest. As Jesus and his disciples passed near Bethany, He decided to visit the home of Martha, which she shared with her brother Lazarus and her sister Mary (Luke 10:38, NRSV). Martha was a woman who knew her place and enjoyed making sure her domain, the home, was just so. Mary, on the other hand, from the time she was a little girl, questioned her assigned role. She was not content to only do the things women were expected to do. She wanted a full range of life experiences. So, when she found out Jesus was coming over, she made a choice for herself.

For most of the day, Mary helped Martha clean, cook, and set up for Jesus and His disciples. When they arrived, she greeted them, offering them water to wash their feet. However, Mary's plans for the rest of the evening violated the traditional role of a woman. She had already decided she would sit down among the disciples to be taught by Jesus (Luke 10:39, NRSV).

Before this day, she had been listening quietly from the sidelines, soaking up as much as possible as she went about doing women's work. She wanted to raise her hand, ask questions, and think out loud about God! She was tired of denying this part of herself; the part Martha did not know and of which she certainly would not approve.

People often like us best when we are exactly what they expect us to be. Even Jesus had to deal with people being offended by who He was. He was not who they remembered Him to be. How did He get so good? He's just a carpenter. Mary's boy! Who does He think He is? (Mark 6:2-4, NRSV)

Martha's sister, Mary, was a woman seeking truth for herself despite societal limitations. Mary's sister, Martha, was offended that Mary had chosen to act outside of the expected norm. Martha was unwilling to revise her expectations of her sister. Can you hear Martha saying, "Who does she think she is?"

Being female places me automatically into the Sisterhood, but there's a lot about sisters I don't understand, perhaps because I don't have any biological sisters. However, I have had relationships with girls and women my whole life, that fall into the sister, friend, and frenemy categories. I also have two daughters from whom I have learned much about the bond between sisters.

My heart rejoices when I see Black women excelling and aches when we stumble, suffer, or attack one another. Rapper, Wale, said,
"Sue me, I'm rooting for everybody that's Black.
I say, sue me, I'm rooting for every
Black woman and girl!
Rooting for us to all succeed!
Rooting for us to love ourselves and
support one another!
Rooting for us to realize we don't have to
compete for a man's attention."

You know that is part of what was happening during the visit right? Martha did not want Mary to monopolize Jesus' time. Rather, she wanted Jesus to be in awe of her hospitality and culinary skills. She did not want Mary distracting Him, all up in his face! So, she threw poor Mary under the bus, thinking Jesus would scold Mary and send her into the kitchen to help. Instead, Jesus democratized spiritual blessing when He announced that by giving Him her undivided attention, Mary had chosen the good part; her access to God would not be blocked. In Jesus' own words, "Martha, Martha, you are worried and distracted by many things; there is need of only one thing. Mary has chosen the better part, which will not be taken from her" (Luke 10:41-42, NRSV).

    Had this situation occurred today, I can just imagine Mary's response to Martha's betrayal being, "Girl, I thought you had my back? My sister of all people is the one to do me in and is the one whose betrayal hurts the most." Mary probably expected one of the disciples to say something against her, maybe even Lazarus, but not Martha! She was the one who stepped in when their parents died, and the one who laughed at her corny jokes when others just shook their heads! This was Martha! Her shining example of womanhood, which she of course rejected. And now, her example of the pain women can cause one another when they don't know how to celebrate the different paths on which women travel.

    Being a woman called to ministry has not been easy, but I have never been more disappointed than to hear women, my sisters, offer the greatest opposition to my answering God's call and using my gifts. Sisters, I thought you would have my back! You are the home crowd that should be cheering for me and other women as we answer God's call! Not booing us because you don't want to revise your expectations and understanding of a woman's place.

Mary decides to deepen her spirituality and Martha is jealous. "Look at Mary, trying to be a man! Who does she think she is?" We started the same, doing the same things that all women are expected to do. What makes her so special? She's no better than me!

What I like about the story is that it ends without resolution. How did the sisters respond to Jesus' pronouncement? Was Martha able to hear what Jesus said? If Martha felt that Jesus showed favoritism to Mary, she might have been resentful and taken it out on Mary once everyone was gone. How did the empowering words of Jesus impact Mary? Were they able to restore or maintain the bond and love that makes the relationship between sisters so special? What do you think?

Author: Rev. Dr. Jill Bradway (she/her)

References

New Revised Standard Bible. (1989). World Publishing. National Council of Churches.

Wale, Price, K., Carter, T., Harmon, WZ, Denton, N., & Wooten, D. (2019, Oct. 11) *Sue Me.* Song by Wale, Songwriters, Price et al., Producer: D. Woo, Rance & Gulledge

MARY Magdalene
— staring e empty tomb

Chapter 13

Mary Magdalene

*"For all have sinned, and come short of
the glory of God;"*
Romans 3:23

The Short Story

Mary Magdalene was born in Magdala in Galilee, hence the name Mary Magdalene. Jesus spent much of his earthly life ministering in Galilee. It is speculated that Mary may have been a prostitute. However, nowhere in the Bible is this confirmed. It is noted by the Jewish Talmud that her birthplace of Magdala was reputed to have been a place where harlotry was openly practiced. In fact, the city of Magdala was eventually destroyed because of its practices (Lockyer, 1976); so, guilt by birthplace? I think not.

It is true that Mary Magdalene was inhabited by seven demons and underwent a demonic cleansing by Jesus (Luke 8:2). For this to happen, it required a deep faith in the Power of Christ with prayer, without magic or rituals. Instead, Jesus used simple commands; and Mary was freed. Her faith had made her free. After her demonic cleansing by Jesus, she walked with Him and became a true believer and devout follower of Jesus Christ. From such lowly beginnings Mary grew in her walk with Jesus to eventually become the first to be in the presence of the risen Lord (Matthew 28:8). Hallelujah!

The Longer Story

Look at what can happen when we faithfully walk in His way!

Sometimes when we cannot clearly see the road ahead, we run into roadblocks and quagmires. We get lost walking along in this world by our own shortsightedness instead of walking in faith. Other times, we walk farther into trouble because we think we can get out on our own. Maybe we don't know that there is a Helper nearby who sees our plight. We keep trying on our own, not realizing that demons have entered in to take advantage of our defenselessness. Mary Magdalene lived in such a state: demons controlled her misery for who knows how many years. Then along came Jesus one blessed day. "Oh, Happy Day!" She who had been inhabited by evil, hurtful, demons and living with sin had a fateful encounter with the Son of God early in His ministry in Galilee. He cleansed her body and soul of seven devils (Mark 16:9). Mary was freed to pursue her own life! From that day forward Mary Magdalene became a faithful follower of Jesus Christ. She travelled with His entourage, learning from His teachings. She was always nearby, watching and rejoicing as He healed the sick and poor in spirit, fed the hungry, healed the blind and lame. Most importantly she listened as He preached the Good News of God's coming Kingdom!

In my mind's eye I see Mary Magdalene as the 13th disciple; one who cooked and cleaned and tidied up (sound familiar, ladies?) and, as with the other women followers, gave unsparingly of her substance, (Luke 8:3) ever busy, ever present, and faithfully listening, learning, and serving her Savior.

Because of her faithfulness God in His amazing grace rewarded her with being present at the final occasions of Jesus' life on earth. This included being a faithful witness at Jesus' Crucifixion (Matthew 27:56), along with Jesus' Mother Mary and John the disciple whom Jesus loved. She was also the first to be in the presence of the risen Lord Jesus Christ (Mark 16:9), who spoke her name in recognition and to whom the angel of the Lord said, "...go quickly, and tell his disciples that he is risen from the dead;" (Matthew 28:7-8). In other words, go "tell it" to the 11 disciples. When she told them that He was alive, and that she had seen Him, she was not believed (Mark 16: 10-13). Such was it and still most likely remains related to the male/female dynamic.

It's tempting to speculate what Mary's life would have been like after that. After the resurrection, there's no more mention of Mary Magdalene in the Bible. However, I imagine her continuing to faithfully preach and teach the Gospel of Jesus Christ.

She most likely acted on His Great Commission to "Go Ye into all the world and preach the gospel to every creature" (Mark 16:15). Rejoice for the Kingdom of God is at hand! Go tell it and sin no more. And that should be the message for all Christian women as we walk forward in faith and love and service to our Lord and Savior Jesus Christ. What do you think?

Author: Gail Chitty

References

King James Bible. (2007). Super Giant Print, Dictionary and Concordance of the Holy Bible. Nashville: Holman Bible Publishers

King James Bible. (2000). Nashville: Holman Bible Publishers

Lockyer, H. (1976). All the Women of the Bible. Grand Rapids: Zondervan Radmacker, E., Allen, R., and Wayne House, H. (2004). Nelson's Compact Bible Commentary, Nashville: Thomas Nelson Publishers, Inc.

Mary - Mother of Jesus

Chapter 14

Mary Mother of Jesus

"Train up a child in the way he should go: and when he is old, he will not depart from it."
Proverbs 22.6 (KJV)

Mary of Nazareth, wife of Joseph, and Mother of Jesus, was a humble Jewish peasant of unblemished character. She was destined to nurture and protect God's divinely chosen child whom she would raise to become a perfect example for Him. Being globally, and interdenominationally known as the Holy Mother of Jesus, makes Mary deserving of the highest recognition and honor. She was the perfect candidate exalted to the highest honor of conceiving and raising God's only son.

Mary a descendant of David is honored in churches and during religious ceremonies when reciting the powerful Catholic prayer, "Hail Mary, Full of Grace, Blessed art thou among women, and blessed is the fruit of thy womb, Jesus (Xavier University). The first part of this prayer, as recorded in Luke 1:28, "...Blessed *art* thou among women," were among the exact words the angel Gabriel spoke when informing Mary that she was God's chosen (Luke 1:26-28). Remarkably, during the past 100 years (1922-2021), Mary has been the highest ranked girl's name chosen for babies born in the United States (ssa.gov).

The first mention of Mary is in reference to her espousal to Joseph and an angel visiting Joseph in a dream reassuring him that marrying Mary, a virgin, was fine, and the child she was carrying was Holy Ghost conceived (Matthew 1:18).

When Gabriel visited Mary in Nazareth, a city in Galilee, he shared God's plans for her to conceive. Mary hastened to remind the Angel of the impossibility, as she had not been with a man (Luke 1:34). Gabriel reminded her of her barren cousin Elisabeth who was pregnant with child at her late age and, "that God made it possible, for with God nothing shall be impossible" (Luke 1:13-24; 36-37).

Mary conceded, God had prepared her womb to carry a son called Jesus who would be so great that He would reign forever, and His kingdom would never end. This child would be miraculously molded into the greatest to ever reign, and even walk among mankind. Mary rejoiced and praised God her Savior, "For He hath regarded the low estate of His handmaiden: for, behold, from henceforth all generations shall call me blessed" (Luke 1:46-48).

Mary was known for her humble submission to the will of God and praised God for favoring her to become the mother of the Messiah. The delivery of Jesus was in an isolated, unassuming town called, Bethlehem in Judaea, the hometown of his earthly father where they had traveled to be taxed. When time drew near, they sought shelter in preparation for the birth but couldn't get lodging at the inn. Jesus, their first born lay in a straw lined, padded manger wrapped in swaddling clothes (Luke 2:4-7). Jesus was undoubtedly, raised to honor his parents, as God requires (Exodus 20:12), and was taught obedience, as Mary was meek and lowly in heart (Luke 1:48).

Ironically, there is no mention of Joseph after the ceremonial Feast of the Passover, where after anxiously searching for their 12-year-old son Jesus in the crowd, found Him teaching in the temple. He promptly dismissed their concern, with that heart-piercing explanatory statement and question, akin to, why are you worried? "Don't you know I must be about my Father's business?" (Luke 2:48-51). I suspect this was painful for both His parents, but particularly His mother as she kept all He said to them in her heart (Luke 2:51). She was undoubtedly, witnessing the unfolding of what Jesus was to become. Joseph was likely dead before Jesus' crucifixion for it is unimaginable that he would not have been present during these two life-changing events (Mark 3:31-35; John 2:1-11, 19-25).

Mary and Joseph had four sons, and several daughters after the birth of Jesus. Not much is known about them, but Jesus had a miraculous life; teaching, healing and working one miracle after another. His first miracle would likely have not occurred, if not for His mother's intervention at a wedding ceremony which Jesus and His disciples attended. Mary informed Jesus that the wine was all gone. He dismissed her. She told the servants that whatever Jesus told them to do--- they should do it.

Jesus eventually asked the servants to take their six water pots, currently containing stone and fill them instead with water. They filled each to the brim with water and presto they had wine. The governor of the wedding believed the cheapest wine is always served after the guests are drunk, but noted that in this case, the best had been saved until the end. The servants, disciples, and Mary all recognized the miracle Jesus had performed.

There is an old church saying indicating that children who don't obey their parents are unlikely to obey God. Obedience was classically demonstrated throughout Jesus' life for which Mary is partly accredited. How would you measure up today? Would you pass the test of obedience to your parents? How about to God?

Mary was at the cross, and in the upper room after the resurrection and ascension of Jesus. The last mention of her was where she appeared at the gathering of women immediately after Jesus ascended to heaven (Acts 1:14). Now widowed, Mary was entrusted to the disciple John (John 19: 27). God knows all and He sees all. Throughout His sojourn on earth and His demise at the cross, there is no doubt that His mother experienced great heartache.

Author: Margie Lovett-Scott

References

King James Bible. (1990). Nashville: Thomas Nelson Publishers, Inc.

United States Social Security Association. Retrieved October 5, 2022 from: https://www.ssa.gov/oact/babynames/decades/century.html

Xavier University. Retrieved October 5, 2022 from https://www.xavier.edu/jesuitresource/online-resources/prayer-index/Catholic-prayers

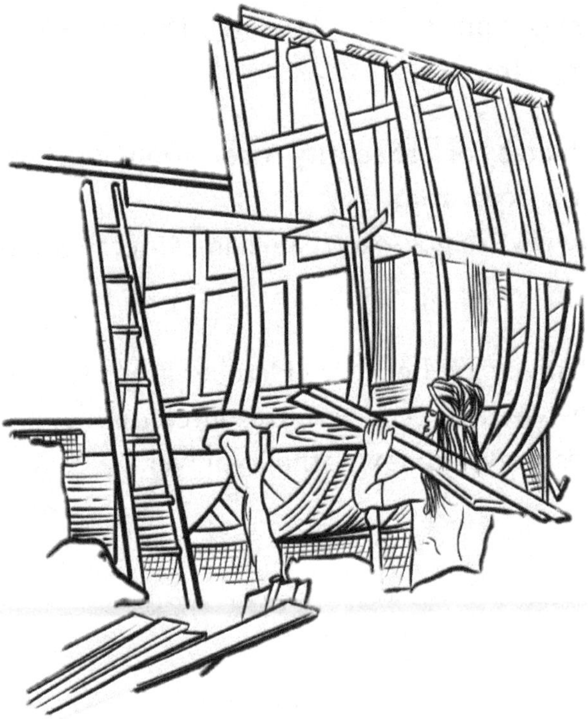

Chapter 15

Noah's Wife

"Don't listen to those who say YOU CAN'T. Listen to the voice inside yourself that says, I CAN."
Shirley Chisolm

The earliest Biblically documented name attributed to Noah's wife is Naamah (Genesis 4:22). Little is known about Noah's sons Shem, Ham, and Japheth. Even less is known about their wives. We do know that their mom survived the flood and exited the ark with seven family members. I liken Noah's wife to a consummate unsung, missionary. Although missionaries who travel globally aiding those in need were typically not gender favored like those in today's Black church, who are generally women. The founding Pastor of my church, a Missionary Baptist Church, taught us that all members of a Missionary Baptist Church are missionaries and are expected to actively engage in mission work wherever needed. He would say, "it matters not whether you wear white on Mission Sunday or are delegated to sit in a designated section of the church, every member is a missionary."

Noah's wife could fittingly be called a missionary. She witnessed her husband diligently going about what the Lord had commanded of him. Noah carefully followed the Lord's instructions for building an Ark exactly as instructed. Although she did not directly participate in the actual building of the ark, one can imagine the supportive role she must have played. No doubt, she offered Noah encouraging words, provided provisions, and fanned or wiped his brow as he worked in the blazing sun. She also, most likely chased away the naysayers and those ridiculing him for building such an enormous vessel on dry land.

The situation may have been laughable for some but not for her. I assume she played the role of helpmate, encouraged her sons and their wives to believe, and finally, and safely assisted in ushering every person and animal safely onto and later off the Ark.

I envision her springing into action as she assisted with caring for all those aboard the ark, and groomed her daughters-in-law, to do the same. Furthermore, she most likely encouraged that they stay on their knees in prayer, while Noah remained in communication with God. Much of what she did during their venture was akin to mission work.

It rained without ceasing for 40 days and 40 nights resulting in the destruction of every living creature on Earth. After disembarking from the Ark, no further Biblical references are made of Noah's wife. One can assume, however, that although God provided all their needs and ensured their safety during their voyage, life as they knew it was forever transformed.

Noah's wife played a significant role in ensuring all seven people who disembarked from the Ark, remained of sound mind and body throughout their time aboard. She needed to make sure that as they arrived on dry land, they were physically and mentally able to carry out their new responsibilities. Notably, "And God blessed Noah and his sons, and said unto them, "Be fruitful, and multiply, and replenish the earth" (Genesis 9:1). God was with them throughout their Ark experience, and once the Lord quieted the waters, and they were able to disembark, I'm sure that wasn't the end of Naamah's story.

We're sometimes thrust into situations where we must follow God by serving the least of His people. No matter the circumstance or need, we're compelled to step up and get the job done. Have you ever been placed in such an intensely, complex and stressful situation whereby you were so entangled you couldn't see your way out? Yet, against all odds, you rose to the occasion and functioned to the best of your capabilities, finally turning the situation around?

I recall having to travel to pick up my dad from his retirement home in Jacksonville, Florida then back to Rochester after cancer had spread to his brain. His illness was manifested by wandering and bizarre behavior. At the time, I was balancing full-time school and work, while caring for four children, the youngest of which was only two years old. My siblings promised to help but couldn't in the end.

Just months earlier I had filed for divorce. Moments after informing my ex-husband that I wanted out of the marriage; he withdrew all but $58 of the more than $12,000 we had in our account. Soon after, checks began bouncing. My life was completely turned upside down. I prayed my way through, and God's miraculous power prevailed, which is when I learned that faithful perseverance pays off. If we press on toward the mark, and have faith in God, we will succeed.

Author: Margie Lovett-Scott

References

King James Bible. (1990). Nashville: Thomas Nelson Publishers, Inc.

Genesis 4:22

And Zil-lah, she also bare Tu-bai-cain, an instructer of every artificer in brass and iron: and the sister of Tu-bal-cain was Na-a-mah.

Priscilla enter to worship

Chapter 16

Priscilla

*"...unto whomsoever much is given,
of him shall be much required."*
Luke 12:48

Priscilla and Aquila are an impeccable demonstration of *couples' ministry* in the first century. Paul recognized them as his "helpers in Christ Jesus" (Romans 16:3). Contextually, "For unto whomsoever much is given, of him shall be much required" (Luke 12:48), Luke's concluding words while speaking to the judge concerning the responsibility of a master chastising a disciple/servant.

God's "much" is demonstrated by giving His only son's life for our benefit, so that we may receive eternal life. There are little Biblical details surrounding the "much" regarding this phenomenal woman named Priscilla. Rather, in this story, we are challenged to interpret between the lines. The word, "much" in this chapter is synonymous with preparation and commitment to achieve the best outcomes in life that honors God.

In terms of Priscilla's life, how exactly do we define "much?" From birth, Priscilla's "much" included preparation and commitment to her vocation which especially included experiences she would have in

Corinth, and Ephesus. Every person has been given a vocation (Ephesians 4:1), which is to live a life that demonstrates the power of God. Priscilla's vocation included being a wife, teacher/preacher, tentmaker, Christian, hospitable, follower, friend, and team member.

Priscilla was a Jew and devout Christian. Her "much" can be summarized by a quick look at Proverbs 31:31, "Give her of the fruit of her hands; and let her own works praise her in the gates." Her home turned into a church was one of the primary results of the "much" in her life coming full circle. Priscilla was among the pillars of faith in establishing the church as saluted by Paul (2 Timothy 4:19).

In Luke 12:48, "... For unto whomsoever much is given, of whom shall be much required: and to whom men have committed much, of him they will ask the more." We find an equation (much given = much required) for life. This equation supports the importance of reviewing one's resume/portfolio, thus summarizing that, which has been accomplished through opportunities provided.

Our lives demonstrate God's providence. Have you ever recognized an "Emperor Claudius" in your life? Someone known for forcing people out of their vocation. How did you handle it? Priscilla chose to leave her vocation in Rome and seamlessly transitioned her tentmaking business to Corinth. Perhaps the market for tentmakers was far more prosperous in the commercial city of Corinth than in Rome.

Ironically, God's providence guided Paul from Athens to Corinth (Acts 18:1). Similarly, God's providence was at work when Emperor Claudius expelled the Jews from Rome, and Priscilla came to Corinth (Acts 18:2). This act allowed Priscilla's home to be prepared to welcome Paul and the first home church.

The "much" given Priscilla included the trade of tent making and her gift of hospitality. I am contending that as a Jewess, Priscilla was very knowledgeable of the Jewish Law as was Paul, and that she had a similar "Damascus Road" experience (Acts 9) as Paul. In retrospect, we can see how Priscilla and Paul were divinely connected. Priscilla, Aquila, and Paul are an impeccable demonstration of team ministry in God's Kingdom.

Priscilla's "much" in hospitality provided encouragement for Paul to remain steadfast and immovable abounding in his vocation (1 Corinthians 15:58). Priscilla's "much" continued moving, best demonstrated by showing responsibility for others. Apollos, with her mentoring became "an eloquent man and mighty in the scriptures," (Acts 18:24-28). Priscilla's "much" allowed her to observe without criticism. When Apollos' was falsely teaching about the baptism of John, rather than openly criticizing him, Priscilla provided an opportunity to meet his need by improving his knowledge of the role of the Holy Spirit. After Priscilla welcomed him into her home, Apollos received her mentoring, thus empowering him to be more effective in spreading the gospel.

Have you ever experienced an Apollos in your life, who after benefiting from your mentoring rejected your "much?" Paul referred to Priscilla as having risked her neck for him. That risk may have included individuals rejecting or opposing her. Subtly, through our passion to give "much," we can generate dust on our feet, resulting in physical and mental abuse. The moral here is not to allow anyone or, anything; family, church, workplace, and/or community, devalue your "much."

Like Priscilla, in our responsibility to serve others, it is incumbent upon us to know when it's time to move on. We're only responsible for extending invitations, not the responses. Our greatest witness here is Jesus, himself. Jesus was omniscient and omnipotent, yet He said, "And whomsoever shall not receive you, nor hear you, when ye depart thence, shake off the dust under your feet for a testimony against them"... (Mark 6:11). God knows the purpose that comes through our "much," and He knows our end. Therefore, from the beginning of life, our "much" begins to ensure that we arrive at our future and expected end. (Jeremiah 29:11). Priscilla did and so can we!

Author: Ruth Wiley-Simmons

References

King James Bible. (1977). Nashville: Thomas Nelson Publishers, Inc.

- **Queen of**
- **Sheba** - crowned and showered with gifts.

Chapter 17

Queen of Sheba

"Don't sit down and wait for the opportunities to come. Get up and make them."
Madam CJ Walker

Though Solomon was known to be a very generous person, he was reportedly exceptionally generous with the Queen of Sheba. In fact, he gave her anything her heart desired!

However, *the half has not been told.* Yes, King Solomon was generous to the Queen of Sheba, but she was also very generous to him. The Queen of Sheba was on a mission and had heard about Solomon and his relationship to the Lord (1 Kings 10:1 NIV). Even as queen, the Queen of Sheba wanted to learn more about what she had heard, and she wanted to meet him for herself and test him with hard questions and riddles (1 Kings 10:1-2 NIV). Not only did she wish to establish potential trade routes between the two countries, the Queen of Sheba also wished to learn more about King Solomon's administrative skills concerning the management of his Kingdom. I imagine she also wanted to know about the God Solomon served and the wisdom God blessed him with to run his kingdom.

Oftentimes, only one side of a story is told without paying attention to what women bring to the table. If the Queen of Sheba had come empty handed, lacking intelligence, power, wealth, and beauty, King Solomon would never have entertained her in the first place. She first had to get in through the palace door before she could see the king, which meant she needed a plan. The Queen of Sheba couldn't sit and wait for opportunity to come to her because that wasn't going to happen. The Queen understood that in order to gain knowledge and obtain what she was seeking, she would have to go to the King and give him something in return. The Queen of Sheba was a shrewd Black woman who ruled the Kingdom of Saba, which scholars believe was Ethiopia or Yemen. (Myths & Heroes PBS, 2008)

The journey from Saba to Israel would've taken several years. However, no distance was too great to obtain the answers she sought. The Queen of Sheba traveled thousands of miles from Northern Ethiopia to Jerusalem by a camel-drawn caravan carrying gold, spices, and precious jewels as well as her servants and clothing. If the Queen was going to be away six to eight years, she could not fail in her mission. The Queen knew that she had to come with her best game plan. I imagine she had to map out how she was going to travel, who would go with her and whom she would leave behind. It was important for her to determine beforehand who she could trust to run her kingdom during her absence. Also, the Queen would have had to study King Solomon, the land of Israel, its resources and what his kingdom needed. All these factors were important in determining what she should bring to the table. Because of the many years it would take to make the journey, the Queen must've believed that the investment of her time, her research, and her kingdom's resources were well worth the trip.

One can only imagine the pomp and circumstance surrounding her arrival. There she was accompanied by her entourage, followed by caravans carrying spices, large quantities of gold and precious stones, her clothing, and her staff's clothing as well. She arrived at King Solomon's door with advisers, make-up artists, stylists, bodyguards, armor-bearers and chefs.

Once he admitted her and she introduced herself, she then asked him "everything she had on her mind and Solomon answered all her questions. Nothing was too hard for the King to explain to her" (1 Kings 10:2-3 NIV). When she was allowed to witness his wisdom, observe his kingdom, his palace, his staff, the temple, his administration, and all that he had, she was impressed (1 Kings 10:4 -7, NIV).

The Queen of Sheba praised King Solomon and told him that all his wealth and wisdom were more incredible than she had imagined. Because of the

Lord's eternal love for Israel, He made Solomon king "to maintain justice and righteousness" (1 Kings 10:9 NRSV). God's love for Israel -- the half had not been told (1Kings 10:4-9 NIV).

"And she gave the king 120 talents of gold (A rough calculation yields 7,920 pounds according to Meeker & Hendren, 2014), and large quantities of spices, and precious stones. Never again were so many spices brought in as those the Queen of Sheeba gave to King Solomon" (1 Kings 10:10 NIV). King Solomon was impressed by her position and wealth, her title, intelligence, and beauty. "King Solomon gave the Queen of Sheba all she desired and asked for, besides what he had given her out of his royal bounty.

Then she left and returned with her retinue to her own country" (1 Kings 10:13 NIV). She left and took all that she had learned, all of Solomon's wisdom and all he had taught her about God. When she arrived home, she implemented and shared what she had learned.

Sometimes, we have to look at the end game, the long-term investment and weigh the cost and the benefits. The Queen of Sheba knew that the journey she was going to make was well worth the time and investment. What investments do we need to make for ourselves, for our families, for our kingdoms/communities? Real investment takes commitment and sacrifice.

     Which trade routes do we wish to establish and what plans do we need to make? How will we get there or accomplish our goal? What are we seeking in our relationship with God and how much time are we willing to spend in establishing an intimate relationship with Him? The Queen of Sheba used everything she had at her disposal. How about us?

     When making life-changing decisions, how often do we weigh the cost against the benefits before deciding? What are we willing to give in order to receive ten-fold for our family and communities? All that the Queen of Sheba gave to King Solomon and all that she received and learned from him, plus everything she did for her people when she arrived back to her kingdom, the half has not been told.

Author: Rev. Kimberly L. Detherage, Esq.

References

Meeker, K., & Hendren, M. (2014, January). The Elusive Queen of Sheba: Gold and Spices/Womenfromthebook Blog. Posted on January 26, 2014 by womenfromthebook. Retrieved on December 14, 2022.

New International Bible. The Pastor's Bible, New International Version, Large Print, Bible, Pastor's Edition. Grand Rapids: Zondervan, (2000).

New Revised Study Bible. The Wesley Study Bible, New Revised Standard Version, Regular Edition. Nashville: Abingdon, (2009).

Public Broadcasting. (2008), Myths & Heroes: The Queen of Sheba. PBS. Retrieved on November 14, 2022https://www.pbs.org/mythsandheroes/myths_four_sheba.html. 2008

Bibliography

Fontaine, Carole R. (December 31, 1999) "Queen of Sheba: Bible." *Shalvi/Hyman Encyclopedia of Jewish Women*. Jewish Women's Archive, from: https://jwa.org/encyclopedia/article/queen-of-sheba-bible, The True Story of the Queen of Sheba, Retrieved on December 14, 2022.

Grunge. (July 24, 2020). *The True Story of the Queen of Sheba*, http://www.youtube.com/watch?v=xydptpstes. YouTube video. Retrieved December 14, 2022.

Rahab

Chapter 18

Rahab

"It doesn't matter who you are, where you come from. The ability to triumph begins with you - always."
Oprah Winfrey

The story of Rahab once again demonstrates how God can use whomever he chooses! Rahab, a Canaanite, was the mother of Boaz who was the husband to Ruth. Her lifestyle resulted in her being widely scorned. Nonetheless, she rose to the occasion and averted a dangerous situation when needed. She had been a harlot with a sinful past. Yet, after being saved by God's grace, she turned her life around. When you have been chosen by God, He will not leave you ill-equipped.

Rahab was a prostitute who saved two spies sent by Joshua to survey Jericho (Joshua 2:1). She was not an Israelite, rather she chose the religion of her mother, a Semite who believed in the law of one God, Jehovah (Burton, 2005). This makes perfect sense as your mother is your first teacher. I can attest to this just by watching my mother. I wanted what she had in her religion. Seeing her God provide so much peace in her life resulted in me wanting that for myself. So, it would behoove me to study and prove her life worthy.

The house in which Rahab lived is described as having been positioned against the town wall with a stairway leading up to the flat side of the roof, almost adjoining it (Lockyer, 1967). This made it possible for visitors to leave discreetly. A blanket spread on the roof could easily provide a hiding place for anyone needing to conceal themselves from a pursuer.

There was also a scarlet, threadlike cord, which we would later learn, allowed Joshua's men to easily slide down from the roof and escape into the mountains by simply following Rahab's instructions. There they would hide out for three days, thus avoiding capture. The scarlet threadlike cord the spies used to scale the wall, would later signal the two spies from Joshua's army to "Go into the harlot's house, and bring out the woman and all that she hath," during the destruction of Jericho (Joshua 2:1-24; 6:22-25).

Rahab was an intelligent woman, who cherished the prayers written on clay tablets that had been given to her by her mother before she transitioned home (Burton, 2005). Justified not only by faith but by works (James 2:24-26), Rahab seized the moment to save her and her father's household (Joshua 2:17-18). When she awakened that morning who knew that she would become part of the lineage of Jesus Christ. You never know when your blessing and gifts will be needed.

I don't believe in happenstance. Instead, we end up being where we are supposed to be, at just the right time. Rahab was making some home improvements, with readily available materials and supplies. Who would have guessed that these supplies would be useful in creating a hiding place and an escape hatch for Joshua's spies.

When the trackers arrived at Rahab's door, she acknowledged that the spies had been there. She convinced them, however, that they had already left by way of the Eastern gate, sending them in the opposite direction. Afterall, the spies were men of God doing His will. Joshua, in following directions to destroy the city of Jericho, was to spare the lives of Rahab and her household. "By faith the harlot Rahab perished not with them that believed not" (Hebrews 11:31). She lived, while the unbelievers died.

The Bible is unclear on a couple of points, leaving one to raise questions as I did. The spies had heard about Rahab and her reputation, which I suspect preceded her. Remember, it is common for some people to make up their minds about you before they meet you. The saying you never know who is watching is very true. In fact, what you do in life is often more important than what you say. Some people claim to be on the right side of God, when behind closed doors they engage in activity that is displeasing to God. Some may call these people hypocrites. Others might excuse and justify such behavior explaining that individuals just do what they must to survive from day to day.

Historically, in the old West, successful women bar owners were suspected of being involved in other unsavory activities. I wonder if Rahab may have been an innkeeper and manufacturer of red linen. However, because it's likely that Joshua's spies knew of Rahab's background, they probably believed she might assist them.

The scripture reveals, "But my God shall supply all your need according to his riches in glory by Christ Jesus" (Philippians 4:19). My next pondering is about the scarlet cord, an indication that it was a house of ill-repute later used to signal that no harm should come to Rahab's house, satisfying the oath the spies had made to her.

In exploring the significance of Rahab's story, we must consider three speculative observations. The first observation is the color red. During Old Testament times, red was used as a sign of faith. As it hung from Rahab's window during the attack from the Israelites, it also represents the color of blood. What connection do you see between this and Jesus Christ?

Also, Rahab found peace in her mother's faith and cherished the prayers on her mother's clay tablet. Where did others in the Bible find peace when they were troubled? How about you? Finally, while the spies were on their mission for three days, they hid in the mountains per Rahab's suggestion. What other event occurred during those three days?

     Regardless of my speculations, God's word is true. Rahab believed the words of the spies with an oath based on God's word. Our God chooses the least expected among us to carry-out His plan. Has He called on you to do anything lately? Whatever your response, just remember when God calls, be sure to answer!

Author: Loretta Madison

References

Burton, A. (2005). Women of the Bible: Rahab's Story. New York: Signet Publishing Group

King James Version. (1970) The Holy Bible. Iowa Falls: World Bible Publishing

Lockyer, H. (1976). All the Women of the Bible. Grand Rapids: Zondervan

Rizpah –
sat watching over slain bodies

Chapter 19

Rizpah

"I have learned that as long as I hold fast to my beliefs and values, and follow my own moral compass, then the only expectations I need to live up to are my own."
Michelle Obama

After the death of Saul, and during the early half of David's reign as king of the breakaway Kingdom of Judah, King David led a battle to avenge the Gibeonites. The Gibeonites were not Israelites, rather remnants of the Amorites that Saul had pursued. David handed over to the Gibeonites the seven bodies of Saul's sons. Rizpah was now mourning the tremendous loss of her two sons, and the loss of her stepdaughter's five sons, but she never gave up. Instead, she stood at the rock of Gibeah, and for five months, watched night and day over their slain bodies preventing vultures and other vicious animals from ripping apart their flesh and destroying any semblance of recognition of who they had been -- no easy task for anyone. There she stood night and day courageously fighting off predators and protecting the remains of these precious bodies and their dignity.

However, it must be noted that the death of Rizpah's sons and Saul's five grandsons did not have to happen. They didn't have to be sacrificed for the wrongs of her husband King Saul, and they did not have to be hung and left for the birds of prey and wild animals to devour.

Rizpah's sons were the pawns of two governments -- King David's and the people of Gibeah. Why were Rizpah's sons sacrificed? At the time, Israel was experiencing a three-year famine. Times were rough and David wanted the famine to stop so Israel could flourish. So, King David inquired of the Lord, and God told him it was because King Saul and his family were guilty of the murders of the people of Gibeah.

King David, wanting to make things better, asked the Gibeonite people what he could do to make it right. They told him they didn't want money; instead, they wanted seven descendants of King Saul handed over to them "to be killed and exposed at Gibeah for Saul—the Lord's chosen one" (2 Samuel 21:6 NIV). David consented and two of Rizpah's sons, Armoni and Mephibosheth, were included in the seven, handed over to the Gibeonites, then executed on a hill, leaving their bodies exposed to stink and rot. (2 Samuel 21:1-10 NIV)

Rizpah was powerless. She didn't have any opportunity to intervene and save her sons. Nor did she get the chance to ask King David if there was perhaps an alternative way out. Had he inquired of God whether the Gibeonite's request, although in line with the Israelite law of retributive justice, was a reasonable one. Her sons' only crimes were that of being heirs of King Saul.

Rizpah's pain and suffering over losing her sons was never even considered in the plan. She had lost her position in society after the death of her husband, King Saul, and her two sons. Women were protected and cared for by the men in the family. Consequently, Rizpah no longer had protection nor resources of her own.

King David didn't even give her sons a proper burial. What Rizpah could not do for them in life, she did in death. She preserved their dignity and highlighted the injustice of their deaths. Our Black mothers today are losing their Black sons through governmental decisions and systemic racism throughout the land. Today, we see this, through the cradle to prison pipeline, the criminal justice system, police brutality, and the senseless killing and demonizing of our sons. Trayvon Martin, Daunte Wright, George Floyd, Ahmaud Arbery, Manuel Ellis, and Tyre Nichols just to name a few.

While Rizpah couldn't prevent their deaths, she would honor them and bring them justice that way. She was going to lament publicly for her sons, and she didn't care about the consequences. It didn't matter to her what she looked like, what people would think of her or how long it would take; it didn't matter if people whispered or called her "Crazy Rizpah." It didn't matter that she might get hurt trying to keep her sons safe and their memories alive.

Rizpah wanted the world to see and take notice of what King David had done to her sons. Similarly, when Mamie Till's son Emmett was brutally beaten and killed for allegedly speaking to a white woman. His body was thrown into a river after he'd been beaten beyond recognition. Mamie Till demanded an open casket viewing because she wanted the world to see her son's ravaged and distorted body. She was determined to shed light on the violent treatment of Blacks in the South.

Rizpah put on sackcloth, a traditional sign of mourning and repentance. I imagine she didn't just lament the death of her sons but also asked for repentance for the acts committed against her children. I also imagine that she trusted in the Lord to see her through to justice.

For six months, (Smith & McCreary), Rizpah stayed with her sons' bodies, advocating on their behalf. Rizpah stayed night and day beating back the buzzards, wild animals and predators from destroying her sons' bodies. She was bent on ensuring that neither their names nor their legacies were tarnished. She did not want the government to spin the wrong story about her two sons. The longer she stayed with the bodies of her sons, the longer the light would be shed on their senseless murders.

More than likely, people thought she would give up after a few days, but one day turned into six months. King David, learning what Rizpah had done, retrieved the bones of King Saul and Jonathon, his son, and gave them a proper burial; he also gathered the bones of Rizpah's sons and the five grandsons of Saul, and they were also buried (2 Samuel 21:11-13 NIV).

It was not until the burials had taken place, that God answered the prayers for their country and ended the famine (2 Samuel 21:14 NIV). God ended the famine not because of the agreement between King David and the People of Gibeah, but only after Rizpah's actions and the proper burial of all the men who had died.

Sometimes, when injustice occurs, or we feel helpless, we must do what we think is right, even when it might not make sense to the world and have costly consequences. We must trust God, believing that He will honor our decisions and our quest for justice.

What injustice have you experienced lately and how did you handle it? Did you ask God to work it out?

How do we follow our own moral compass during the many situations we face? How do we not compromise our values even when we feel powerless? How do we speak up? How do we put into action our moral values despite systemic racism and sexism?

Author: Rev. Kimberly L. Detherage, Esq.

References

New International Bible. (2000). *The Pastor's Bible.* New International Version, Large Print Bible, Pastor's Edition, Grand Rapids: Zondervan.

Smith, T.A. & McCreary, M.L. "Rizpah: Tragedy into Triumph." In: "She is Called Women of the Bible Study Series." Vol. 1, Reformed Church Press, pp. 73-80.

Bibliography

Clark-Soles, J. (2020). *Women in the Bible*. Interpretation. Westminster John Knox Press.
Dunn, B. (June 02, 2021). "Who Was Rizpah and What Does Her Story Teach Us about the Importance of Grief?" www.Biblestudytools.com.

Smith, T.A. & McCreary, M.L. (2020). "Rizpah: Turning Tragedy into Triumph: One Woman's Vigil for Justice" In: *She Is Called - Women* of the Bible Study Series., Vol. 1, Reformed Church Press, pp. 73-80. Rizpah: Turning Tragedy into Triumph | Women of the Bible Study Series Women of the Bible Study (faithward.org).

RUTH AND NAOMI

Chapter 20

Ruth

"Small acts of goodness can have a lasting impact."
Queen Elizabeth II

Ruth, an awesome example of love, redemption, devotion, loyalty, hard work, and determination. She trusted wholeheartedly in the LORD God in the era of the judges. Her unwavering commitment to carrying on after the loss of her husband, and her brother-in-law, was expected to result in her demise. However, for 10 years Ruth had been observing her mother-in-law and marveled at her faith.

Ruth sensed there was something different about the unseen God Naomi worshipped compared to the gods of the Moabites. Ruth had most likely heard Naomi praying and praising her GOD even though she was in a strange land. Perhaps she heard her pray aloud, *"Behold I am with you and will keep you wherever you go and will bring you back to this land; for I will not leave you until I have done what I have spoken to you"* (Genesis 28:15).

When Naomi announced that she was going back to Bethlehem, Ruth refused to stay behind in Moab. Her mind was made up, her answer nonnegotiable. Naomi was her family now and she would not leave her side short of death. So, they both took their faith journey together hoping to reintegrate into a society that would be vastly different than the one Naomi had just left.

Now Ruth would be a stranger in a culture she knew nothing about. But Naomi's God had a purpose for Ruth and her loyalty and obedience would be rewarded. We know how the story ended. How marvelous for the world that Ruth is now named in the genealogy of our Lord Jesus Christ (Matthew 1:5).

Could you be as courageous and loyal as Ruth and give up everything you know, family, friends, your job, and your homeland? Well, my story was directly impacted by her words. My corporation convinced me seven years before to take my daughter and move to another state. I did, leaning on my faith even though I really didn't grasp the totality of all it really meant. So, I was well ensconced in my new life when I learned some disturbing news from back home.

My Ma, (Daddy's second wife), had suffered several strokes and the last one left her completely dependent on my father. He was no longer the caregiver she needed, so when I discovered he had sold their home and was moving to Alabama, I was terribly upset. When she first got sick, I hadn't relocated yet, and I begged her to come live with me, but she wanted to stay with Daddy, hmmmm!

On my final visit to my childhood home, a somewhat inebriated guest of theirs, whom I'd never met, was talking with them but suddenly looked across the kitchen table at me and quoted this scripture: *"Entreat me not to leave you, or to turn back from following after you; for wherever you go, I will go; and wherever you lodge, I will lodge..."* (Ruth 1:16). I didn't grasp what he meant until I was driving back to my home in Virginia.

I called back to Ma and asked, "Do you want me to go to Alabama with you?" She answered, "yes!" Then I sold my house and moved to Alabama. I've often said, it's hard to relocate the first time because there are so many unknowns, but once you do it, subsequent moves are so much easier. In fact, I've moved way too often, but through it all, the Lord Jesus Christ has been with me all the way. He truly is the only one I can always depend on.

The many times I've been taught, heard preached, and studied Ruth and Naomi's story, I never imagined how those words would change my life. As I made sacrifices over the years to try and help somebody, "my village" has been many women in the communities where I have lived, who mothered me so I would never feel alone. What a debt I owe. How about you? Who will be your Naomi, even if it's not a total sacrifice? As the song says, "If I can help somebody as I pass this way, then my living shall not be in vain." Amen.

Author: Cheryl A. Pough

References
King James Bible. (1994). Nashville: Thomas Nelson Publishers

Ruth 1:16

And Ruth said, Intreat me not to leave thee, *or* to return after following after thee: for whither thou goest, I will go, and where thou lodgest, I will lodge: thy people shall *be* my people, and thy God my God.

Sarah:

Chapter 21

Sarah

"But when I found that I knew not only that there was a God but that I was a child of God, when I understood that, when I comprehended that, when I internalized that, ingested that, I became courageous."
Maya Angelou

Sarah, wife of Abraham, was unable to conceive and fulfill her dream of having a son. Though believing her plight was to remain barren for life, God miraculously answered her plea. In utter disbelief, she was blessed at age 90 to become the mother of Isaac. This was in fulfillment of a promise God made to Abraham, that Sarah would be the mother of nations and would conceive and bear a son. Sarah's journey between the "she would conceive and bear a son" prophecy and the birth of Isaac, lasted 25 years.

Notably, Sarai and Abram were pagans (unbelievers) who encountered God when He called Abram to leave his home and go to Canaan (an unknown land), (Genesis 12). Abraham was faithful and Sarai being a submissive, obedient wife, obeyed God, took their family and traveled to Canaan. When they arrived in Canaan, God spoke to Abram again, and promised to give his offspring the land of Canaan (Genesis 12:1-3).

While on the journey towards Canaan, Sarai had various encounters with God. Each meeting taught her more about God's power, His character and faithfulness. Sarai witnessed the power of God when He rescued her after she'd been taken by the Egyptians to become the wife of the Egyptian Pharaoh, (Genesis 12: 10-17). She witnessed God destroy Sodom and Gomorrah yet save her nephew Lot and his family (Genesis 19:23-29). Then Sarai witnessed God's power again when King Abimelech took her to be his wife and God closed the wombs of the women of Gerar, forcing the King to release her (Genesis 20: 2-18).

These experiences should have made it clear to Sarai that God protects His people. The Bible tells us: "The Lord shall preserve thee from all evil: he shall preserve thy soul" (Psalm 121: 7). Nothing was going to stop God's plan for Sarai's life, because she had a vital part in His divine plan.

Although Sarai believed in God, she was not sure how he would deliver his promise to give her a son. Sarai and Abram waited 10 years for God to fulfill His promise of a son. Now at 75 years old, and Abram 85, she felt she was too old to conceive and give birth. Besides, fertility was the cause of great distress in the world of the Old Testament. Husbands could divorce their wives and replace them with a surrogate or even adopt a child if the wife could not conceive.

Although, fertile women made fun of infertile women, even despised them (Genesis 16:5), Sarai out of desperation, offered her handmaid Hagar to be surrogate mother to their son. Abraham agreed and Hagar conceived. She gave birth to a son they named Ishmael (Genesis 16).

Sarai's decision to enlist a surrogate turned out to be the worst decision she could have made. It caused pain and suffering between Sarai and Abraham and Hagar and Sarai hated one another. The trouble began when Hagar conceived. Hagar treated Sarai as if the roles had reversed; she acted like the wife. In return, Sarah mistreated Hagar, and blamed Abram for the situation in which they found themselves.

While it must have been very difficult for Sarai to face the trials bought on by choosing to interfere with God's plan, she persevered, and her faith grew stronger. God showed up, blessed her and her faith and gave her the strength to conceive. It had been 25 years since God had promised her a son. Sarai interrupted God's plan, but she didn't change it.

Like Sarai, many of us have interrupted the plan God may have had for us. While impatiently waiting for an answer from Him, we jump headfirst into a situation, do it our way, fail, and more often than not, make the situation worse. How do you handle insurmountable problems?

No matter what our plans are, God's plans will always prevail. He is a promise keeper! "For all the promises of God in him *are* yea, and in him Amen', unto the glory of God by us. Who hath also sealed us and given the earnest of the Spirit in our hearts" (2 Corinthians 1:20:22).

Sarai, who became known as Sarah is listed in Hebrews Chapter 11 as one of God's heroes of Faith.

"Through faith also Sarai herself received strength to conceive seed and was delivered of a child when she was past age, because she judged him faithful who had promised" (Hebrews 11:11).

Author: Yvonne Marshall

References

Allen, RB. (1997). Hagar and Ishmel. In: Thomas Nelson Study Bible. Nashville: Thomas Nelson, Inc

King James Bible. (1997). Study Bible. Nashville: Thomas Nelson Publishers, Inc.

Genesis 16:2

And Sarai said unto Abram, Behold now, the Lord hath restrained me from bearing: I pray thee, go in unto my maid; it may be that I may obtain children by her. And Abram hearkened to the voice of Sarai. And Sarai Abram's wife took Hagar her maid the Egyptian, after Abram had dwelt ten years in the land of Canaan, and gave her to her husband Abram to be his wife.

Chapter 22

Tabitha - also called Dorcas

Acts of the Apostles 9:36-41

"And he gave her his hand, and lifted her up, and when he had called the saints and widows, presented her alive."
Acts 9:41, NKJV

Tabitha, also called Dorcas, was a disciple who lived in Joppa during the time of the Acts of the Apostles. Tabitha is her Hebrew/Aramaic name and Dorcas is the Greek equivalent (Youngblood, 1986). Tabitha is the only woman in the Acts of the Apostles referred to explicitly as a disciple (Newsom & Range, 1992). Tabitha was an important person in the Christian community at Joppa. She was known for her great acts of charity and for her almsgiving. She made clothes for the widows and tended to the needs of the poor. Tabitha did all these things with her own resources.

It has been suggested that Tabitha was a widow and a woman of great financial resources. If her great resources weren't her own, she may have had access to funds because of her connections with those who did (Youngblood, 1995).

When Tabitha became ill and died, the whole Christian community mourned her loss, especially the widows who were the subject of her love and care. They experienced the loss so deeply that they sent for Simon Peter, the Apostle, to come quickly, believing he could heal Tabitha. Peter arrived and went straightaway to see Tabitha. After speaking to her, she was revived. He then presented her back to the community alive.

Joppa

Joppa was a walled city approximately 30 to 35 miles northwest of the city of Jerusalem. It was a seaport city on the Mediterranean serving the city of Jerusalem (Youngblood, 1986). According to the Old Testament, Joppa was part of the territory inherited by the tribe of Dan during the conquest of the Promised Land (Joshua 19:46; Youngblood, 1986).

Joppa was also the home of Simon the Tanner with whom the Apostle Peter spent many days after his healing of Tabitha (Acts 9:43). Today, Joppa is called Jaffa in modern Israel and is surrounded by the city of Tel Aviv.

The Community of Goods

At the point we are introduced to Tabitha, many Christian communities had already been established outside of the regions near and around Jerusalem. Each local Christian community adopted the same model of living established with the first communities. That model was structured so that every member of the Christian community had all things in common.

They sold their possessions and goods and pooled them so that they could be distributed among everyone in the community. This ensured that no one would be lacking what they needed. They worshipped together and lived together as family. Because of this the Lord would add to the communities daily and the Christian communities grew (Acts 2:44-47). Each Christian community also adopted the Old Testament model for the care of widows, orphans, sojourners among them, and the poor.

Reflection

A challenging discovery made during my study on Tabitha, is how many commentators have glossed over her story. The tendency was to use it as a backdrop for the stories of healing attributed to Simon Peter. Peter's vision on the rooftop of Simon the Tanner's home can be found in Acts, Chapter 10.

It was somewhat frustrating because as is often the case, women's stories in many Bible commentaries, do not get the attention like their male counterparts do. Women whose stories do get lots of attention are usually considered exceptional and/or phenomenal, like Deborah, Esther and Mary the mother of Jesus. Additionally, many women's stories, just like Tabitha's, only get attention in association with the main character in the story, usually a male. This discovery only made me more determined to talk about Tabitha.

Tabitha, as a personality in the Bible, is important for several reasons. First, she is the only woman in the Acts of the Apostles referred to as a disciple. This means that her great works characterize her as a model of discipleship for both men and women. Tabitha was well honored in her community because of her great charity work in the Christian community in Joppa. She was a Christian icon in the community at Joppa and was so well honored, that upon her death, the community sent representatives to Simon Peter to come quickly to heal her.

Tabitha was a woman of great compassion and love for the Christian community, especially for the widows. She offered her gift as a seamstress and her own financial and other resources for the care of the community. She took the idea of all in the community having all things in common seriously. Tabitha was very much about doing, not just talking about doing.

It's important to emphasize again that Tabitha offered her gifts to the community. By doing this, Tabitha offered them up as a sacrifice to God. They were her offering in worship as she demonstrated her love for Jesus the Christ. She had become a dedicated and committed believer.

Imagine the time and resources it must have taken for her to provide the level of care she provided in the community. Envision the level of energy and personal physical sacrifice it must have taken for Tabitha to provide the ministry she so freely gave.

Lessons Learned from Tabitha

- ❖ Our gifts and skills were given to us to glorify God and to do great works to His glory.
- ❖ We are not to hoard our resources nor use them only for selfish reasons.
- ❖ There are many times when the Lord expects us to be responsible for the care of the community.
- ❖ As women we cannot always expect recognition, but we can expect that God will provide for us as we care for others, even to the point of healing us of physical and other infirmities.
- ❖ We do not need to be suspicious, embarrassed, or afraid when the community of believers wants to praise us for our good works.

How about you? What gifts and skills has the Lord given you, and in what ways do you use these gifts/skills to glorify Him?

Author: Rev. Dr. J. Esther Rowe

References

King James Bible. (1986). Nashville: Thomas Nelson Publishers

Newsom, C.A. & Ringe, S.H., Eds. (1992). The Women's Bible Commentary. Louisville: Westminster John Knox Press.

Youngblood, RF., Gen. Ed. (1995). Nelson's New Illustrated Bible Dictionary. Completely Revised and Updated Edition. Nashville: Thomas Nelson Publishers, 1986

Bibliography

Henry, M. (1961). Commentary on the Whole Bible. Grand Rapids: Zondervan.

Pfeiffer, C.F. and & Everett, F.H., Eds. (1962, 1990). The Wycliffe Bible Commentary. Chicago: Moody Publishers.

Wall, R.W. (2002). The Acts of the Apostles. In: The New Interpreter's Bible. Vol. X. Nashville: Abingdon Press.

The Servant Girls:

Chapter 23

The Servant Girls

"Woman by Design, Woman on Purpose: A Catalyst to Value Your Voice & Walk in Your Worth!"
Dr. Renee Allison

She Speaks

Peter's hypocrisy was challenged by two servant girls. Although a devoted disciple, when Jesus was taken away, Peter repeatedly, denied he knew Him. Two lowly servant girls, who were sure they recognized Peter as a follower of Jesus, confronted him repeatedly, yet he continued to deny knowing Jesus (Mark 14:66-72).

However, when Peter was below in the palace, along came one of the maids assigned to the high priest. Upon seeing Peter warming himself, she immediately pointed him out as one of the men who'd been with Jesus of Nazareth (Mark 14: 66-67). Not only did Peter deny being with Jesus he denied even knowing what she was talking about. So, he blew her off and walked away. When he reached the porch, the cock crowed (Mark 14:68). Again, a maid saw him and alerted those standing nearby that Peter was one of the men who had been with Jesus. Peter quickly denied it a second time, but upon further observation, those who'd gathered around agreed, that he was one of the men. Not only did Peter look like a Galilean, he also, spoke like one.

He continued, vehemently denying it, and this time he even lost his temper. He began swearing repeatedly saying, he had no idea who this man was with whom they allegedly saw him (Mark: 69-71). The cock crowed again, and Peter immediately remembered Jesus telling him he would deny Him three times before the cock crowed twice, and he began to weep (Mark 14:72), as though remorseful.

Amazingly, two lowly servant girls, who had most likely been raised to always tell the truth, upheld their upbringing, and did not bite their tongue. Rather, they spoke out, and triggered Peter into a state of humility just by speaking up. They'd no doubt seen Peter before because they recognized him right away and called him out. Interestingly, it wasn't until the assembled crowd validated what the girls said, and after the cock crowed, did Peter feel remorse, remembering Jesus' words to him.

How often have we women had something important to say in the presence of others, but were deliberately overlooked, and not given the recognition we deserved? Our voices have been too often silenced in our society. Consequently, even when invited to speak out, many of us are intimidated and reluctant to do so because of past experiences.

Our voices deserve to be heard. These servant girls recognized Peter from previous encounters, perhaps while they were serving the same God. Both had something to say and didn't hesitate to boldly speak out. When we have something important to say, we must be persistent in letting others know, and oh yes make sure they listen.

Like the servant girls, don't get so complacent, and content with the status quo, that you allow yourselves to be dismissed by the Peters of this world. Don't become content with being ignored, shoved off, steamrolled, silenced or disrespected! Rather, when necessary, like the servant girls, speak out with intention and bravery. After all, their voices became the catalyst that triggered a prophetic biblical event!

How amazing that God used servant girls to humble Peter so much that he wept. It fulfills the scripture that Peter would deny Jesus three times before the cock crowed twice. Sometimes women must disturb the peace, make some noise, and bring what I call, "good trouble." God can use any of us in whatever status to be a changemaker. Let us lift our voices every opportunity we get and become catalysts for change!

Author: Rev. Patricia Rector-Hollomon

References

King James Bible. (2019). Super giant print reference Bible. Nashville: Holman Bible Publishers, Inc.

The woman @ the well – woman drawing water @ the well

Chapter 24

The Woman at the Well

"The kind of beauty I want most is the hard-to-get kind that comes from within, strength, courage, dignity." -- Ruby Dee

The story of "The Woman at the Well" has always intrigued me. Who was this woman? They don't give us her name in the Bible, but we do know that she encountered Jesus at Jacob's well. He made one request of her and drew her into deliverance sparking the beginning of her ministry.

"There cometh a woman of Samaria to draw water: Jesus saith unto her, 'Give me to drink.' (For his disciples were gone away unto the city to buy meat) How is it that thou, being a Jew, askest drink of me? ... For the Jews have no dealings with the Samaritans" (John 4:7- 9). Unaware of who had asked her for a drink, she discussed some of the reasons why just the very act of her giving Him the water He requested was unlawful, unreasonable, and unacceptable.

She let the stranger know she was aware of the social norms, and religious boundaries that would be crossed in this one act of giving Him water. She also, wanted Him to be aware that she was in no way docile or uninformed. She, like many women, had been perceived as unthinking or unlearned of the things for which only men were privy. The perception of weakness and women being of lesser value, held them in a second-class status, only slightly greater than the cattle that men owned. Yet, she spoke strongly to the stranger at the well, as if to say, "I'm not as weak as you believe I am!" Sparring with Jesus, word for word she sought to prove her point that she was not the empty vessel that she may have been accused of being.

It was then that Jesus makes her aware of His knowledge of the laws and related religious connotations. In fact, He delves into a more personal level of her existence, perhaps touching a deeper part of her soul. Skillfully, Jesus withdrew from the secret well of her soul. "Jesus saith unto her, Go, call thy husband, and come hither" (John 4:16) He had turned the conversation toward her real issue. He wanted to let her know that He knew all about her sins. He wanted her to face the thing she had blocked from her mind. Before this, their conversation had been wading in shallow waters, but now Jesus was leading her into depths she'd been carrying deep within her soul. "The woman answered and said, I have no husband" (John 4:17).

Because He was a stranger, she felt she could speak honestly to Him. Afterall, He was obviously not from around there, and maybe He hadn't heard all the rumors that circulated around town regarding her background. Sometimes meeting someone new gives us the opportunity to reinvent ourselves. She spoke the truth to Jesus, and He affirmed her with His answer:

Jesus said unto her, "Thou hast well said, 'I have no husband:' For thou hast had five husbands; and he whom thou now hast is not thy husband: in that saidst thou truly" (John 4:17-18). Simply put, "You are right when you say you have no husband. The fact is, you've had five of them and the man you now have is not your husband. So, what you just said is quite true."

    Jesus wanted to free her from the heavy burdens she carried. Instead of looking upon her with disdain, He affirmed at that moment that she was speaking truthfully. He caused her to feel that there was something good about her. He didn't wag his finger at her or hail accusations toward her. Rather, He acknowledged her openness, and her willingness to speak honestly to Him.

    Was having five husbands really a crime? Should she have been ashamed because she had married five times? Not really! To marry was the way of the culture. A woman without a husband was vulnerable, and without provision. To have a husband meant more than having a companion or a lover; it meant having a legacy, a lineage, a heritage. Perhaps, fearing the judgment of others caused her not to marry the man with whom she currently lived. She probably figured, married or not, neither choice would stop the ridicule she suffered.

    The relief she sought in the six men never came

to pass, but it was in the Seventh Man, Jesus the Christ that she found her deliverance. Seven is the number of completion and signifies she was released from her burden and set free from the shame. So much so, that she ran back to the city and told others about Jesus saying, "Come see a man who told me all things that I ever did: is not this the Christ?" (John 4: 28-29:39) She was in such a hurry to tell others about Jesus that she left her water pot behind, no longer concerned about the shame she felt.

She wanted to tell others about The Messiah, who knows our deeds, yet doesn't condemn us. This was the beginning of a powerful ministry she carried out telling others about the Seventh Man, Jesus Christ. Jesus did for this woman what earthly men couldn't do for her. He healed her heart.

I believe that the miracle in this story was that Jesus talked to her. He allowed her to express her thoughts. The release she felt, possibly occurred because, finally a man spoke to her and offered her something valuable and eternal instead of asking for something from her. Jesus knew everything about her, yet still offered her a drink of *living water*, quenching her thirst forevermore. He was the only man who could draw from her what was so deeply needed.

I personally thank Jesus, for this story. It reminds me of my own. When my husband died, it left a gaping hole in my soul. Over and over, and for many years, I have tried to heal myself. As a woman it is not acceptable to have multiple relationships that eventually end, leaving us alone, yet again. People unjustly think there's something wrong with a woman who can't keep a man. But is it my fault that I loved my husband so much, that when he died it left a huge hole in my heart?

So, like the woman at the well, I continued my daily routine of carrying the waterpots, secretly hoping that one day the right man would come along. He'd give me water that quenches that burning desire for love and acceptance most women want. In the meantime, until then, and forever more, I am glad that I have Jesus who knows everything that I have ever done, and yet He fills me with Water that springs up into everlasting life. So, again, I thank Jesus for this story. Hopefully, you will too!

Author: Evangelist Sherry Barton

References

King James Bible. Retrieved: November 10, 2022, from https://www. biblegateway.com/version/King-James-Version-KJV-Bible/

Bibliography

Lockyer, H. (1976). All the Women of the Bible. Grand Rapids: Zondervan

Woman w/the issue of blood -

Chapter 25

The Woman with the Issue of Blood

"Don't ever make decisions based on fear. Make decisions based on hope and possibility. Make decisions based on what should happen, not what shouldn't."

Oprah Winfrey

Close Enough

Many know the story of this woman, as referenced in the Books of Mark and Luke. "And a certain woman, which had an issue of blood twelve years, and had suffered many things of many physicians, and had spent all that she had, and was nothing bettered, but rather worse, When she had heard of Jesus, came in the press behind, and touched his garment... and she felt in her body that she was healed of that plague..." (Mark 5:25-34); "And a woman having an issue of blood twelve years, which had spent all her living upon physicians, neither could be healed of any, came up behind *him,* and touched the border of his garment: and immediately her issue of blood was stanched" (Luke 8:43-44).

For 12 long years she suffered with a bleeding disorder that labeled her unacceptable in her community. She had not set out to be ostracized. In fact, the Bible tells us she reached out to those she thought would be able to help her, including medical professionals. How devastated she had to be when she found out that her condition only worsened by their hands, leaving her in financial ruin.

Not only had she invested her money; she had invested in all her dreams. Now, physically and emotionally depleted, she heard that a man named Jesus was passing through her town. She thought to herself, "if only I can get close enough."

Have you ever been sick and tired of being sick and tired? This woman was totally, exhausted. She had placed her faith in the wrong people, and life was being sucked right out of her. She was dying when the truth was, she wanted to live. Her life was not desirable, and she was ashamed.

Embarrassment and pain have a way of shaming us to the point of isolation and despair. But, on that day, she realized that if she got close enough to touch Jesus, everything would be all right. She had a made-up mind, and nothing was going to stop her, nope, not that day.

Ladies, when we place our hopes and desires in the wrong men, they eventually deplete us. How emotionally draining it is to believe you have the best when you really have the worst. The natural hemorrhage of this woman signifies her emotional spend down. No doubt she was ashamed and housing feelings of unworthiness. Each betrayal of trust pulled her deeper and deeper into imprisonment in a living hell.

Selah

I've known the Lord since I was a little girl. My grandmother made sure I went to church with her. Some Sundays appeared never-ending. Each week began with early morning Sunday school and extended all the way to Sunday evening Singing Concerts known as *Sang-Ins*! I always felt really good in church. Everything about it felt right. As I got older, and started dating, I began attending church less and less. I associated feeling good with being good (for me) and so when I fell in love with Tony, I proclaimed, "Look what the Lord has done!" Instead, I became entangled in what I know now to be a soul tie.

I hadn't heard the term *soul tie* until I became a young adult. I had never heard of this concept and like many of us, I've dated a few men in my day. It seems I fell in love every four or five years. Who really counts when love is involved? Each relationship became more and more physically and emotionally draining. I had come to the end of my rope and felt emotionally depleted. It was then that I remembered what I had heard as a little girl in Sunday school. I remembered Jesus was passing by.

Like the woman with the issue of blood, I reached out to touch Him. No one else needed to know. This was between Jesus and me. Excuse me sir, excuse me ma'am, but I need to get to Jesus! I went unnoticed by many, but noticed by the One that matters the most. Jesus was called to action by the sincerity of my faith. I have learned that my faith is the catalyst to my healing. I was on a mission. I was desperate for change, and like this woman, I remembered Jesus. Crawl, lie down and roll, do whatever you have to do to make it to Jesus. I pressed through the crowd of all the fine, well-off men, and got close enough to touch the man that matters most. His name is Jesus.

Author: Elder Sheila Rogers

References

King James Bible. (1990). The Holy Bible. Nashville: Thomas Nelson Publishers, Inc.

Mark 5: 32-33

And he looked round about to see her that had done this thing. But the woman fearing and trembling, knowing what was done in her, came and fell down before him, and told him all the truth.

Vashti-
Crowned queen:

Chapter 26

Vashti

"One of the lessons that I grew up with was to always stay true to yourself and never let what somebody else says distract you from your goals."

Michelle Obama

Queen Vashti was a woman of integrity. Her refusal to appear before her husband, King Ahasuerus, "to shew the people and the princes her beauty, for she was fair to look upon," at a feast at Shushan the palace, resulted in the King divorcing her and marrying another young virgin, Esther.

Queen Vashti's actions cost her everything, her home, her court, her position and her reputation in the land. Bible annotations throughout the New Testament, suggest that God never intended for husbands to **rule** their wives. But let's look a little closer at the circumstances of her life.

Vashti was a trailblazer, though she hadn't envisioned that role for herself. She most likely knew the consequences she would face for disobeying the king. Yet, she took a stand and refused to flaunt her beauty in front of assembled men, knowing it was the right thing to do, even in her day.

We're unsure if she knew the identity of the men around the king, but Memucan in particular, fearing other women would be influenced by Vashti's actions (Esther 1:14-18), told the king, "For this deed of the queen shall come abroad unto all women, so that they shall despise their husbands in their eyes, when it shall be reported." (Esther 1:17) But history clearly records that she set things in motion, in the atmosphere, which is still impacting the lives of women today, more than 25 **centuries** later!

It's been 200 years since abolitionist Harriett Tubman, though born into slavery, refused to adhere to a slave mentality. She stood up against wrongdoings towards women and decided that when the laws and masters were wrong and in direct violation of God's Law, she would fight for what was right. She vowed to act on what she believed to be fair, leaving the ultimate victory to the Lord.

Many women, old and young, have taken similar stands for what they believe in, refusing to bend to pressure. Have you ever taken a stand, contrary to a societal norm? Perhaps standing up for yourself in the workplace or maybe you've challenged religious norms. I did, though I didn't know the extent of what it would cost me until I was involuntarily laid off, fired!

I returned to Rochester, New York to accept a job I really didn't want. The hiring manager was known for taking care of his people, but a close teammate encouraged me to come on board because he needed my mainframe and printing systems expertise on his team. So, I came back to Rochester and started my career. The manager promised that when a position became available for the product I wanted to work on, it would be assigned to me.

That's not what happened, however. Organizations change, teams change, and new managers have commitments to their own people. My integrity, my honesty and keeping my word were viewed as flaws. In this case, I interfered with the closing of a quarter-million-dollar equipment sale because I told a customer the current software was inadequate for their application.

Looking back, it was one of the best decisions I've made. I learned that I didn't have to lie or compromise who I am, and still am; one who plans to live, to thrive, and be successful. Also, knowing WHOSE I am makes all the difference.

As my exit process was unfolding, I already knew I was getting laid-off. My team held protected status because of the work we did throughout the United States. However, I was the only team member called to a "meeting" when the organizational news broke. When my team and associates throughout the company heard, they commented, "who did Cheryl exasperate?" They knew my level of integrity and that I would not allow myself to bow down to pressure despite the consequences.

I can honestly say that my decision to stand firm has not been a significant hindrance these past 28 years. Though I went a little too far in declaring I would never work for another corporation, I was not seriously concerned because I stand on the following: "And we know all things work together for the good to them that love God, to them who are the called according to His purpose." (Romans 8:28) As for me, things indeed worked and continue to work together for my good.

The Scriptures don't tell us anything more about Vashti. In fact, she's not even given a line in Unger's Bible dictionary other than under Ahasuerus, "Divorces Vashti." (Unger's Bible Dictionary, p. 31) Ephesians 5:25 states, "Husbands love your wives, even as Christ also loved the church, and gave himself for it;" King Ahasuerus let his royal advisers influence him to decree an unalterable law when he was in no condition to make a wise decision. (Esther 1:10) How different could Vashti's story have been had the king waited until the next morning!

How many women and men have suffered great losses because others in leadership made decisions that negatively impacted their lives? I shared my story and how my life was altered, but I also want to tell you that even when you own part of the responsibility for what happens in life, stay true to yourself, and live with what God allows. After all, "... my God shall supply all your need according to his riches in glory by Christ Jesus."

(Philippians 4:19) It's a future promise, and He has indescribably glorious riches!

Author: Cheryl A. Pough

References

King James Bible. (1994). Nashville: Thomas Nelson Publishers, Inc.

Unger's Bible Dictionary (1985). Chicago: Moody Press

Chapter 27

Summary

A Final Look Back!

You've heard the stories of 22 of the women mentioned in the Bible. How will you use this information to which you've been introduced or reintroduced? We've shared but a snapshot of these stories from the perspective of Christian sisters. These women have lived experiences that shed light on the stories of the Biblical women highlighted in this book. How you utilize this information may provide insight into your own story, and reaffirm lessons learned along your own Christian journey. As you apply these stories to your own experiences, you may find answers that shed light on where to go from here.

Perhaps you'll share these stories with your family and friends. Or maybe you'll find them worthy enough to share in your book clubs, women's groups, or even expand your discussions into an existing or expanded Bible study. You might become inspired to delve into the stories of other Biblical women, those not covered in this book. There may be a woman in the Bible who is perhaps more reflective of your own life's journey. Whatever route you take in further studying women in the Bible, remember that during Biblical times women were powerless to change the course of their lives. Making mistakes, and being afforded a second, or third chance was literally not an option.

Today, we are saved by grace and covered by the blood of Jesus Christ, so we have choices. We can change the trajectory of our lives, as we walk with the Lord and find our purpose. We are free to discover what He is truly directing us to do.

We all make mistakes, sometimes repeatedly. We repent, and are given opportunities for a do over, time and time again. Today, unlike during our Biblical sisters' days, Jesus shed his blood on the cross so that we might have a second chance to get it right. But, for His grace and mercy, where would we be? How many do overs will it take for us to finally get where we know we must?

Far too often, when things are going well, we lose sight of how we got there and slip back into old habits. Some of us get so caught up in our trials that we shake our fists at God, and even turn our backs on Him. We profess to love the Lord. We ritualistically call out His name during times of thanksgiving, dire need, and even before making major decisions. We never hesitate to have personal conversations with Him when trouble comes, or when we're faced with major life challenges. But be mindful of the fact that we must stay on the Christian battlefield until our lives, and our personal stories are reflective of God's love.

We strive daily to do that which is pleasing in God's sight until our lives are, finally, a living testimony to His love. We are encouraged to reflect on these things and decide how we might best apply the stories in this book as we work toward embracing God's true purpose for our lives.

Author: Margie Lovett-Scott

References

Allen, RB. (1997). Hagar and Ishmel. In: Thomas Nelson Study Bible. Nashville: Thomas Nelson, Inc.

APA Editorial board. (2020). Publication Manual of the American Psychological Association: The official guide to APA Style. 7th edition. Washington DC: American Psychological Association.

Bond, SE. (2017, Oct. 24). The hidden labor behind the luxurious colors of purple and indigo. Retrieved November 26, 2022, from hyperallergic.com: https://hyperallergic.com

Burleigh, H.T. (1927). *Deep River.* New York: G. Ricordi and Co.

Cartwright, M. (2016, July 21). Tyrian purple. Retrieved November 4, 2022, from World History Encyclopedia: https://www.worldhistory.org

Chisholm, T. (1923). Great is Thy Faithfulness, Song. Hope Publishing (Based on Lamentations 3:23)
Crowder, Stephanie Buckhanon, When Momma Speaks.
Culpepper, R.A. "The Gospel of Luke," In: The New Interpreter's Bible. Volume IX. Nashville, TN: Abingdon Press, 1995, pp 3-490.

Fort, C. (2011). What the Bible says about creating Vision Boards + An expressive therapeutic art prompt.

Retrieved November 14, 2022, from https://12tribesministries.com

Green-Brown, C. (2016, January 12). Visual prayer: How to create a spiritual Vision Board. San Diego: Dream Life Foundation

Isaak, K. (2020, January 20). Should Christians make Vision Boards and set goals? Retrieved November 4, 2022, from https://love motherblog.com/podcastepisode20/

King James Bible. YouVersionBibleApp (2016). Edmond: Life. Church. Downloaded. November 2017.

King James Bible. (2007). Super Giant Print, Dictionary and Concordance of the Holy Bible. Nashville: Holman Bible Publishers

King James Bible. (2000). Nashville: Holman Bible Publishers

King James Bible. (1997). Study Bible. Nashville: Thomas Nelson Publishers, Inc.

King James Bible. (1994). Nashville: Thomas Nelson Publishers, Inc.

King James Bible. (1990). Nashville: Thomas Nelson Publishers, Inc.

King James Bible Online. (1987). Retrieved November 29, 2022, from https://www.biblegateway.com

King James Bible. (1977). Nashville: Thomas Nelson Publishers, Inc.

King James Bible. (1971). Nashville: Thomas Nelson Publishers, Inc.

King James Bible. (n.d.) Retrieved: November 10, 2022, from https://www. biblegateway.com/version/King-James-Version-KJV-Bible/

Liefeld, W.L. "Luke," In: Gaebelin, Frank E., Gen. Ed. The Expositer's Bible Commentary. Volume 8. Grand Rapids, MI: Zondervan, 1984, pp 818-1059.

Lockyer, H. (1976). All the Women of the Bible. Grand Rapids: Zondervan

McClain-Walters, M. (2015). The Deborah anointing: Embracing the call to be a woman of wisdom and discernment. Lake Mary: Charisma House Book Group

McGee, V. J. (1981). Thru the Bible, Vol. I, Nashville: Thomas Nelson Publishers.

Meeker, K., & Hendren, M. (2014, January). The Elusive Queen of Sheba: Gold and Spices/Womenfromthebook Blog. Posted on January

26, 2014 by womenfromthebook. Retrieved on December 14, 2022.

New International Bible. (2000). *The Pastor's Bible.* New International Version, Large Print Bible, Pastor's Edition, Grand Rapids: Zondervan.

New King James Bible. (1986). Nashville: Thomas Nelson Publishers

New Revised Standard Bible. (1989). World Publishing. National Council of Churches.

New Revised Study Bible. The Wesley Study Bible, New Revised Standard Version, Regular Edition. Nashville: Abingdon, (2009)

Newsom, C.A. & Ringe, S.H., Eds. (1992). The Women's Bible Commentary. Louisville: Westminster John Knox Press.

Olesen, J. (2013). Color meanings – The power and symbolism of colors Retrieved November 2, 2022 from https://color-meanings.com

Packer, J.I., and Tenny, M.C. eds. (1980) Illustrated Manners and Customs of the Bible. Nashville, TN: Thomas Nelson Publishers.

Public Broadcasting. (2008), Myths & Heroes: The Queen of Sheba. PBS. Retrieved on November 14,

2022https://www.pbs.org/mythsandheroes/myths_four_sheba.html. 2008

Radmacker, E., Allen, R., and Wayne House, H. (2004). Nelson's Compact Bible Commentary, Nashville: Thomas Nelson Publishers, Inc.

Roe vs. Wade, 410 U.S. 113, United States Supreme Court. January 22, 1973.

Ryan, J. (2021, June 16). 7 Lessons we can learn from Deborah in the Bible. Retrieved September 10, 2022, from https://www.crosswalk.com/faith/bible-study/lessons-we-can-learn-from-deborah-in-the-bible.html Schaberg, J. "Luke," In: Newsom, Carol A and Sharon H Ringe, Eds. The Women's Bible Commentary. Louisville: Westminster/John Knox Press, 1992, pp 275-292.

Smith, T.A. & McCreary, M.L. "Rizpah: Tragedy into Triumph." In: "She is Called Women of the Bible Study Series." Vol. 1, Reformed Church Press, pp. 73-80.

Spangler, A. and Syswerda, J.E. (2007). Women of the Bible. Grand Rapids: Zondervan.

Tenney, M.C., Gen. Ed. The Zondervan Pictorial Encyclopedia of the Bible. Volume 5 Q-Z. Grand Rapids: Zondervan, 1975, 1976.

Trigilio, J. and Brighenti, K. (2005) Women in the Bible for Dummies. Hoboken: Wiley Publishing, Inc.

Unger's Bible Dictionary (1985). Chicago: Moody Press

United States Social Security Association. Retrieved October 5, 2022 from https://www.ssa.gov/oact/babynames/decades/century.html

Wale, Price, K., Carter, T., Harmon, WZ, Denton, N., & Wooten, D. (2019, Oct. 11) *Sue Me.* Song by Wale, Songwriters, Price et al., Producer: D. Woo, Rance & Gulledge

Xavier University. Retrieved October 5, 2022 from https://www.xavier.edu/jesuitresource/online-resources/prayer-index/Catholic-prayers

Youngblood, RF., Gen. Ed. (1995). Nelson's New Illustrated Bible Dictionary. Completely Revised and Updated Edition. Nashville: Thomas Nelson Publishers, 1986

Bibliography

Burton, A. (2005). Women of the Bible: Rahab's Story. New York: Signet Publishing Group

Clark-Soles, J. (2020). *Women in the Bible.* Interpretation. Westminster John Knox Press.

Dunn, B. (June 02, 2021). "Who Was Rizpah and What Does Her Story Teach Us about the Importance of Grief?" www.Biblestudytools.com.

Fontaine, Carole R. (December 31, 1999) "Queen of Sheba: Bible." *Shalvi/Hyman Encyclopedia of Jewish Women.* Jewish Women's Archive. Retrieved November 14, 2022, from https://jwa.org/encyclopedia/article/queen-of-sheba-bible, The True Story of the Queen of Sheba, Retrieved on December 14, 2022.

Grunge. (July 24, 2020). *The True Story of the Queen of Sheba,* http://www.youtube.com/watch?v=xydptpstes. YouTube video. Retrieved December 14, 2022.

Henry, M. (1961). Commentary on the Whole Bible. Grand Rapids: Zondervan.

King James Bible. (2019). Super giant print reference Bible. Nashville: Holman Bible Publishers, Inc.

King James Version. (1970) The Holy Bible. Iowa Falls: World Bible Publishing

Lockyer, H. (1976). All the Women of the Bible. Grand Rapids: Zondervan

Pfeiffer, C.F. and & Everett, F.H., Eds. (1962, 1990). The Wycliffe Bible Commentary. Chicago: Moody Publishers.

Smith, T.A. & McCreary, M.L. (2020). "Rizpah: Turning Tragedy into Triumph: One Woman's Vigil for Justice" In: *She Is Called - Women* of the Bible Study Series., Vol. 1, Reformed Church Press, pp. 73-80. Rizpah: Turning Tragedy into Triumph Women of the Bible Study Series Women of the Bible Study (faithward.org).Wall, R.W. (2002). The Acts of the Apostles. In: The New Interpreter's Bible. Vol. X. Nashville: Abingdon Press.

Chapter Contributors: Alphabetically Listed

Sherry Barton, Rochester NY
Evangelist
Lead Medical Secretary
Vocalist, Praise and Worship Leader
Woman at The Well Convener,
Zion Hill Missionary Baptist Church
"Charm is deceptive and beauty fleeting, but a woman who fears the Lord is to be praised." Proverbs 31:30

Rev. Dr. Jill Bradway (she/her), Wilmington, DE
Interim Pastor, Silverside Church
Solopreneur, Jill Bradway & Associates LLC.
Transformative Interculturalist
Womanist Practitioner, and Ministry Professional.
"Creating a more intercultural space, one person, one conversation, one interaction at a time."

Gail Chitty, Gates, NY
Retired Physical Therapist
Health Ministry Co-Convener & Past President
Library Ministry
Zion Hill Missionary Baptist Church
"God is able; God is Good."

Rev. Kimberly L. Detherage, Esq., East Elmhurst, NY
Pastor, Attorney, Dean, Consultant, Presenter
Author, Educator & Spiritual Director
St. Mark A.M.E. Church, Pastor
"The thief comes to kill, steal and destroy. I came that you might have life and have it more abundantly."
---John 10:10

Martha Hope, Brighton, NY
Radio Talk Show Host
Founder & CEO of Senior Expressions, Inc.
Mental Health Advocacy for Adult Seniors
Mentor for young adult women
President, Rochester Genesee Valley Club
Business and Professional Women,
A Founding member of Christian Friendship
Missionary Baptist Church, Henrietta NY
"Faith does not make the struggles of life disappear. It makes the struggle easier to bear."

Dr. Corrine Houser, Rochester, NY
Christian Educator
Black Cultural Heritage Devotee
Entrepreneur
Zion Hill Missionary Baptist Church.
"The joy of the Lord is my strength."

Dr. Margie Lovett-Scott, Rochester, NY
Published Author
Nurse Educator, Professor Emerita
Health & Library Ministry
Zion Hill Missionary Baptist Church.
"Striving each day to do what is pleasing in God's sight."

Loretta Madison, Rochester NY
Missionary
Mission Treasury, Finance Retiree
Zion Hill Missionary Baptist Church
"Using my daily grace to become the person, my God entrusted me to be."

Yvonne Marshall, Rochester, NY
Finance Secretary
President Pastor's Aide
Member Board of Elders,
Zion Hill Missionary Baptist Church
"Nothing is impossible with God, He always, delivers on His promises."

Joanne Mitchell-McLaren, Royse City, Texas
Nurse Practitioner, Patient Engagement Liaison
Royse City, Texas,
In Christ New Hope Ministry, Rochester, NY
"The mountain can be moved but you must Believe to Receive."

Cheryl A. Pough, Rochester, NY
Mother
Former Bible Study and Sunday School Teacher,
Contributor, World Evangelism Ministries
"For the law of the Spirit of life in Christ Jesus hath made me free from the law of sin and death." Romans 8:2

Rev. Patricia Rector-Hollomon, Rochester, NY
Associate Minister
Health and Wellness Ministry, Chair
New Bethel CME Church
"Give me O' Lord a servant's heart, that I may serve with Joy!"

Elder Sheila Rogers, Rochester, NY
Ordained Elder, John Maxwell Leadership Team
Faith Community Nurse
Nurse Educator/Mentor,

Mental Health First Aider,
Chaplain Northeast Region/Chi Eta Phi Sorority, Inc.
New Born Fellowship Church
"If it's not in your Heart, it won't be in your Hands."

Rev. Dr. J. Esther Rowe, Rochester, NY
Bible Centre of Rochester & Syracuse:
Instructor of Systematic Theology, Black Theology and Christian History; Mentor
Zion Hill Missionary Baptist Church:
Library Ministry Convener, Christian Education Ministry, Health Ministry and Black History Month Committee
"For I am persuaded, that neither death, nor life, nor angels, nor principalities, nor powers, nor things present, nor things to come, nor height, nor depth, nor any other creature, shall be able to separate us from the love of God, which is in Christ Jesus our Lord."
Romans 8:38-39

Dr. Deborah C. Stamps, (she, her, hers)
Henrietta, NY
Healthcare Diversity
Nurse Executive,
Educator,
Mentor
International Speaker
Trustee and Health Ministry
Chair Genesee Baptist Church, Rochester, NY
"In everything give thanks: for this is the will of God in Christ Jesus concerning you." 1 Thessalonians 5:18

Easter G. Tucker, Pittsford, NY
Sunday School Teacher over 50 years,
Missionary
Trustee chair
Member: Chi Eta Phi Sorority, Inc.,
Black Nurses Association,
NAACP, NCNW
Community and church boards and ministries
Retired nurse administrator
First Genesis Baptist Church, Rochester, NY
"A woman with purpose, productivity, and a devout Christian."

Minister Ruth Wiley-Simmons, Gates, NY
Ordained Minister
LMSW (therapist)
Trustee Board member
Sunday School & Bible Study Teacher
Women's Ministry Overseer
One Faith World Ministries, NASW-NY Chapter
Upper Room Family Worship Center
"Obeying God to thrive, NOT sacrificing to survive."

Bernard Lewis Jr. Illustrator, Tulsa, Oklahoma
Instagram: **artxsaint lewis_bj@yahoo.com**

Alphabetically Listed Scriptural Index

Book of Acts Acts 1:14 Acts 2:44-47 Acts 9:41; 43 Acts 16:14 Acts 18:1-2; 24-28	**Book of Corinthians** 1 Corinthians 15:58 2 Corinthians 1:20:22	**Book of Deuteronomy** Deut. 25:5-10 Deut. 26:12 Deut. 31:12
Book of Ephesians Ephesians 4:1 Ephesians 5:25 **Book of Esther** Esther 1:14-18 Esther 2:7, 15 Esther 4:16	**Book of Exodus** Exodus 20:12 **Book of Galatians** Galatians 4:22-31	**Book of Genesis** Genesis 1:28 Genesis 2: 22-23 Genesis 4:22 Genesis 9:1 Genesis 12:1-3, 10-17 Genesis 16:1-3; 5; 11-12
Book of Genesis Genesis 1:28 Genesis 2: 22-23 Genesis 4:22 Genesis 9:1 Genesis 12:1-3; 12: 10-17 Genesis 16:1-3; 5; 11-12	**Book of Genesis** Genesis 19:23-36 Genesis 20:1-18 Genesis 21:12-20 Genesis 28:15 Genesis 38:11	**Book of Hebrews** Hebrews 11:1 Hebrews 11:11; 11:23 Hebrews 11:24; 11:31 Hebrews 13.5
Book of Isaiah Isaiah 41:10 **Book of James** James 2:24-26 **Book of Jeremiah** Jeremiah 29:11	**Book of John** John 2:1-11 John 2:19-25 John 4:7-9 John 4:16-18 John 4: 28-29 John 4:39 John 19:27 **Book of 1 John** 1 John 1:9	**Book of Joshua** Joshua 2:1-24 Joshua 6:22-25 Joshua 19:46 **Book of Judges** Judges 4:4-9 Judges 5:5; 5:31 Judges 6:15

Book of Kings	Book of Luke	Book of Mark
1Kings 10:1-3; 10:4-10 1Kings 10:13 **Book of Lamentations** Lamentations 3:23	Luke 1:13-24; 26-28; 34, 36-37; 46-48 Luke 2:38 Luke 2:48-51 Luke 8:2-3; 43-44 Luke 10:38-42 Luke 12:48	Mark 3:31-35 Mark 5:25-34 Mark 6:2-4:11 Mark 14:66-72 Mark 16:9; 16: 10-15
Book of Matthew Matthew 1:5; 18 Matthew 5: 9; 13 Matthew 6:34 Matthew 27:56 Matthew 28:7-8	**Book of Philippians** Philippians 4:13; 19 **Book of Proverbs** Proverbs 22.6 Proverbs 31:31	**Book of Psalms** Psalm 34:8 Psalm 68:5 Psalm 121: 7 **Book of Romans** Romans 8:28 Romans 16:3
Book of Ruth Ruth 1:16	**Books of Samuel** 1 Samuel 1:10-11; 17 1 Samuel 2:21 1 Samuel 23:13 1 Samuel 24: 1-11 1 Samuel 25:3-19 1 Samuel 25:14-24 1 Samuel 25:39-42	

Made in the USA
Monee, IL
28 February 2025